CW01639363

Contents

CONTENTS

Introduction

How and when to assess

This Assessment Book provides teachers' notes and a photocopiable pupil assessment sheet for each unit (or group of units) of the programme. This structure gives complete flexibility to the teacher over how and when to assess.

You may decide to use the tests as a check-up for the whole class at the end of each unit.

You may decide, every few weeks, to photocopy the relevant sheets to make a 'mini-test' that can be administered either to the whole class, groups or targeted individuals.

The questions on the test are usually styled in a different way to the other practice materials in Abacus (i.e. Textbooks and Photocopy Masters). Your daily interaction with a pupil along with their work from the practice materials will always provide the first evidence of whether he or she has particular difficulties or strengths. The assessment sheets are designed to probe a pupil's deeper understanding, presenting them with unfamiliar contexts and styles of question. The aim of the Abacus approach is to produce pupils who are confident mathematicians, and who can tackle a variety of contexts and styles, building on what is familiar to them.

Within each teacher's section, the notes are organised under the following headings:

➤ **Skills assessed**, giving details of the exact mental and written skills covered in the unit. Key skills are the focus of the test.

➤ **Diagnostic materials**, detailing particular sections of the Textbook that directly practise the key skills identified above. These pages can be used in two ways:

- as a check of whether a particular pupil is ready for the test
- as further evidence of achievement.

➤ **Oral questions**, several questions that should be read out by the teacher at the start of the test. Answer boxes are provided on the assessment sheets. When administering the test, read each question twice, allowing about ten seconds between each reading. If you are using several different sheets as one test, you can either select a particular question from each sheet, or read out all the oral questions, with pupils recording their answers on a separate piece of paper.

➤ **Common difficulties**, giving advice on the kinds of common mistakes that pupils make, and how to remedy these.

➤ **Practice activities**, further practical activities focusing on the key skills, for pupils who need some further reinforcement.

➤ **Follow-up materials**, where to go next for pupils who have particular difficulties or strengths.

➤ **Answers** to each test are also provided.

Each assessment sheet has a margin on the right, where you can record a pupil's score on each question. This can then be transferred to the foot of the page, and carried over, if appropriate to the next sheet. Where pupils have answered incorrectly, but shown some understanding or relevant working, you may decide to award half a mark.

Administering the tests

An introductory page for the pupils is provided on page 5, so that you can photocopy this each time a test is administered.

No calculators are required for any of the assessment sheets, and any other special equipment needed is specified in the Teachers' notes. The style of administration, e.g. formal, timed, or informal, untimed is entirely up to the individual teacher, and may be decided on a unit by unit basis. Each pupil assessment sheet will take between five and ten minutes.

Before starting, remind the pupils to read each question carefully. The assessment sheets are deliberately uncluttered and pupils can make use of any available space to work out the answer.

Tell the pupils that if they have difficulty with one of the questions to move on to the next one – they can always return later. If they finish the test they should always go back and check their work (if you are timing the pupils, you may wish to build in some time for this).

National Curriculum Levels

The assessment sheets can be used in a variety of ways (either one sheet at a time, or grouped together), and for this reason it is difficult to allocate particular levels to pupil's test scores.

Clearly, it is impossible to assign a level from one test sheet in isolation, and no doubt different pupils will achieve at a higher or lower level on different topics during the year. If, every few weeks, a selection of sheets is administered as one test, then over the course of the year it will become clear whether particular pupils are consistently achieving at a high or low level.

On the whole, the assessment sheets test what it would be reasonable to assume the majority can achieve during Year 5 (P6) (i.e. revising level 3, mainly level 4 or consolidating level C, mainly level D in Scotland).

Sensible decisions can therefore be made about pupils who regularly achieve very highly on the assessment sheets (e.g. consistently achieving 80–100% across a range of topics), those who fall into the 'middle' category (e.g. consistently in the band 60–80%) and those who have difficulties with a range of topics (e.g. consistently achieving less than 60%). You will need to make these judgements in conjunction with your everyday working knowledge of the particular pupil, and their strengths and weaknesses. You are in a unique position to decide if a test result is a 'one-off', or evidence of consistent achievement.

Instructions

- You do not need a calculator for any of the questions on these sheets.
- Work carefully through the questions.
- If you cannot do one of the questions, go on to the next one. You can come back to it later.
- When you have finished, go back and check your work.
- Read each question carefully before trying to answer.
- Use any space on the sheet to work out the answer.

Numbers to 1 000 000

Skills summary

- To read and write whole numbers
- To recognise the value of each digit in whole numbers
- To compare and order whole numbers
- To use the notation < and > when comparing whole numbers

Diagnostic materials

Number Textbook 1, page 3, questions 1 to 10

- Check pupils can combine thousands, hundreds, tens and units and write the numbers formed.

Number Textbook 1, page 4, questions 1 to 10

- Check pupils can write in figures numbers given in words including numbers where zero is a place holder.

Oral questions

1. Write the number 13 456.
2. What is one more than 25 679?
3. (Hold up cards showing 100 000, 40 000, 6000, 50 and 2.) Write the number formed by combining these numbers.
4. (Write 576 340 on the board.) What is the seven worth in this number?

Common difficulties

Pupils can have difficulty recognising the value of each digit. Use a place-value chart to build up numbers by pointing to each part, e.g. 3000, 400, 50, 7, asking the pupils to read the numbers as you point to them. Then use place-value cards to combine the number so they can see how it is written.

Pupils can confuse the greater than (>) and less than (<) signs. It is important to provide opportunities for pupils to read number sentences using these signs as a class as you point to the parts of the sentences.

Practice activities

1 Pick five place value cards: a ten thousand, a thousand, a hundred, a ten and a unit card. Write down the number formed in figures and then in words.

2 Pick six digit cards to form a 6-digit number. Write down the number. Swap two of the digits around and write the new number. Write a greater than or less than sign between the two numbers that have been made.

Answers

1. 13 456	**2.** 25 680	**3.** 146 052	**4.** 70 000
5. 253 614	**6.** 5 000 423	**7.** 304 672	**8.** 812 061

9, **10**, **11** and **14** should be ticked

Name ______________________________ **N1**

1. ☐ **2.** ☐ **3.** ☐ **4.** ☐

/4

Underline the number in figures that matches the number in words.

5. Two hundred and fifty-three thousand, six hundred and fourteen — 2 530 614   253 000 614   253 614

6. Five million, four hundred and twenty-three — 50 423   5 000 423   500 423

7. Three hundred and four thousand, six hundred and seventy-two — 3 004 672   304 672   34 672

8. Eight hundred and twelve thousand and sixty-one — 812 061   81 261   800 1261

/4

Tick the number sentences that are correct.

9. 53 672 < 53 762 ☐

10. 75 018 > 71 058 ☐

11. 809 273 < 908 273 ☐

12. 362 555 < 352 565 ☐

13. 561 914 > 651 914 ☐

14. 1 290 013 < 1 290 031 ☐

/6

Score: ☐ /14   Total: ☐

Rounding

Skills summary

- To round any number up to 10 000 to the nearest ten
- To round any number up to 10 000 to the nearest hundred
- To round any number up to 10 000 to the nearest thousand

Diagnostic materials

Number Textbook 1, page 8, questions 14 to 20
- Check pupils can round a 4-digit number to the nearest 10 or 100.

Number Textbook 1, page 9, questions 1 to 10
- Check pupils can round 4-digit numbers to the nearest 1000.

Oral questions

1. Round 7459 to the nearest thousand.
2. What is 3085 to the nearest hundred?
3. Write 8067 to the nearest ten.
4. How many is 2356 from the nearest ten?

Common difficulties

Pupils often find it more difficult to round up than to round down as when rounding down the ten, hundred or thousand is already given. Pupils can become confused when rounding to the nearest hundred or thousand if they round to the nearest 10 first, e.g. they round 747 to 800, because rounding to the nearest ten produces 750 which is then rounded to 800. Reinforce understanding of rounding by using a number line to provide an image for pupils to see clearly which number a given number is closest to.

Practice activities

1. Roll a dice four times to create a 4-digit number. Round it to the nearest ten, nearest hundred and nearest thousand.

2. Pick four cards from a set of 0–9 number cards. Try and arrange the digits so they form a number that can be rounded to 3000 or 5000 or 7000. Write down the number formed and the thousand it can be rounded to.

Answers

1. 7000 **2.** 3100 **3.** 8070 **4.** 4

5. join 3278 and 2612 to 3000, join 4369 and 3906 to 4000, join 4621 and 5034 to 5000, join 5503 and 6345 to 6000, join 7004 and 6970 to 7000

6, **7** and **8** should be ticked

12 and **13** should be ticked

Name ______________________________ **N2**

1. ☐ **2.** ☐ **3.** ☐ **4.** ☐

/4

5. Join the numbers to the thousand they should be rounded to.

3278 4621 6970 4369 5503

3000 4000 5000 6000 7000

3906 6345 2612 7004 5034

/10

Tick the numbers that have been rounded correctly to the nearest 10.

6. 3029 → 3030 ☐

7. 7546 → 7550 ☐

8. 6123 → 6120 ☐

9. 2365 → 2360 ☐

/4

Tick the numbers that have been rounded correctly to the nearest 100.

10. 1051 → 1000 ☐

11. 4246 → 4300 ☐

12. 3879 → 3900 ☐

13. 7118 → 7100 ☐

/4

Score: ☐ /22 Total: ☐

Multiplication and division

Skills summary

- To recall multiplication facts up to 10 × 10
- To derive division facts corresponding to tables up to 10 x 10
- To express a remainder as a fraction
- To round up or down after division as appropriate

Diagnostic materials

Number Textbook 1, page 12, questions 1 to 16

- Check pupils can use their knowledge of multiplication and division facts to complete missing number questions.

Number Textbook 1, page 13, questions 1 to 12

- Check pupils can calculate remainders after division.

Oral questions

1. What are six lots of seven?
2. Ginny has 17 sweets, which she shares out equally with her two friends. If they each get five, how many sweets are left over?
3. What is 25 divided by 4? Write the remainder as a fraction.
4. A box holds four cakes. I have to put 18 cakes into boxes. How many boxes do I need?

Common difficulties

Pupils often have difficulty learning multiplication facts if they are not aware of the connections between them, e.g. to work out four times a number they could double two times the number etc. As a starting point it is useful for pupils to learn certain facts, e.g. the ×5 table, square numbers. They can then use these facts to work out other facts, e.g. if I know 7 × 7 I can work out 7 × 8; if I know 5 × 8 I can work out 6 × 8.

Some pupils understand division only as sharing and not as grouping, i.e. 24 ÷ 4 is read as 24 shared between 4 rather than how many lots of 4 in 24. Encourage pupils to develop understanding of division as grouping by prompting them to work out division facts by counting in steps of the divisor, i.e. 4, 8, 12, 16, 20, 24 , keeping count on their fingers that 'there are six 4s in 24'.

Practice activities

1 Roll two ten-sided dice. Multiply the two numbers together and write down the answer. Repeat until ten numbers have been written down. Roll the dice again. If the two numbers rolled have a product equal to one of the numbers written down, cross out that number. Repeat until all the numbers are crossed out.

2 Pick a 2-digit number card between 20 and 50. Roll a six-sided dice (if a one is rolled roll again). Write down the division and the answer with any remainder as a fraction.

Answers

1. 42 **2.** 2 **3.** $6\frac{1}{4}$ **4.** 5

5. join a to f, b to g, c to e, d to h

6. 17, 38 and 45 should be circled

7. 3 **8.** 5 **9.** 2 **10.** 6 **11.** 7 **12.** 4

Name ______________________________ **N3** **N4**

1. [ ] **2.** [ ] **3.** [ ] **4.** [ ]

/4

---

5. Join the calculations that have the same missing number.

a $7 \times \_\_\_\_ = 42$

b $8 \times \_\_\_\_ = 56$

c $\_\_\_\_ \times 5 = 40$

d $\_\_\_\_ \times 9 = 81$

e $24 \div 3 = \_\_\_\_$

f $36 \div \_\_\_\_ = 6$

g $21 \div \_\_\_\_ = 3$

h $45 \div \_\_\_\_ = 5$

/4

---

6. Circle the numbers below that give a remainder of 3 when divided by 7.

13 17 23 26 38 45

/3

Complete these calculations.

7. $25 \div \_\_\_\_ = 8\frac{1}{3}$

8. $34 \div \_\_\_\_ = 6\frac{4}{5}$

9. $29 \div \_\_\_\_ = 14\frac{1}{2}$

10. $47 \div \_\_\_\_ = 7\frac{5}{6}$

/4

Find the answer to each problem.

11. There are 4 chairs at each table. There are 27 children in a class. How many tables are needed?

______

12. 18 children are being taken to a football game in cars. Each car can take 4 children. 18 children need a lift. How many cars are full?

______

/2

Score: [ ] /17 Total: [ ]

Halving and doubling

Skills summary

- To derive quickly doubles of all numbers to 100 and the corresponding halves
- To derive quickly doubles of all multiples of 10 to 1000 and the corresponding halves
- To recognise the relationship between multiplication and division

Diagnostic materials

Number Textbook 1, page 16, questions 1 to 9
- Check pupils can double 2-digit numbers.

Number Textbook 1, page 19, questions 1 to 10
- Check pupils can write the division that corresponds to a given multiplication.

Oral questions

1. What is half of 148?
2. I am thinking of a number. I halve it and the answer I get is 36. What number did I start with?
3. A number multiplied by 4 gives an answer of 84. What is the number?
4. If 81 divided by 3 is 27, what is 27 multiplied by 3?

Common difficulties

Pupils can make mistakes when doubling numbers if they do not recognise the value of the digits. They might double 24 correctly as it does not require them to bridge a 10 but they would find double 26 more difficult. Use place-value cards to encourage pupils to partition numbers into tens and units before doubling.

Pupils who find it difficult to see the relationship between multiplication and division may find images useful to support them, e.g. to demonstrate 3 × 14, show pupils three lots of 14 cubes, then put them together; to show 42 ÷ 14 divide the cubes into towers of 14 again. Using the language '3 lots of 14' for multiplication and 'How many lots of 14 in 42?' for division also helps to develop the connection.

Practice activities

1 Pick a 2-digit number card from number cards 10–99 and write down the double (but not the original number). When ten numbers have been written down, work down the list and halve each number.

2 Pick a 2-digit number card between 11 and 20 and roll a six-sided dice (if one is rolled roll again). Write down the multiplication formed, e.g. 15 × 4, calculate the answer, and write three more number sentences to join the first one, i.e. 4 × 15 = 60, 60 ÷ 4 = 15, 60 ÷ 15 = 4.

Answers

1. 74 **2.** 72 **3.** 21 **4.** 81

5. reading from the left: 96 152 89 640 540 360 470

6. 51 ÷ 17 = 3 **7.** 130 ÷ 26 = 5 or 130 ÷ 5 = 26 **8.** 168 ÷ 24 = 7 or 168 ÷ 7 = 24

9. 20 × 7 = 140 or 7 × 20 = 140 **10.** 4 × 41 = 164 or 41 × 4 = 164

11. 3 × 77 = 231 or 77 × 3 = 231

Name ______________________________ **N5** **N6**

1. [ ] **2.** [ ] **3.** [ ] **4.** [ ] 4

5. The function machine doubles numbers that are put into it. Complete the table showing the 'output' and the 'input' of the machine.

Input	48	76		320	270		
Output			178			720	940

7

Complete each division using the multiplication shown.

6. 3 × 17 = 51 ____ ÷ 17 = ____

7. 5 × 26 = 130 130 ÷ ____ = ____

8. 7 × 24 = 168 ____ ÷ ____ = ____ 3

Write a multiplication using numbers from the division shown.

9. 140 ÷ 7 = 20 ____ × ____ = ____

10. 164 ÷ 4 = 41 ____ × ____ = ____

11. 231 ÷ 3 = 77 ____ × ____ = ____

3

Score: ____ /17 Total: ____

Fractions

Skills summary

- To use fraction notation including mixed numbers
- To convert a mixed number to an improper fraction and vice versa
- To recognise when two simple fractions are equivalent

Diagnostic materials

Number Textbook 1, page 23, questions 1 to 10

- Check pupils can use fraction notation to write improper fractions as mixed numbers.

Number Textbook 1, page 25, questions 1 to 9

- Check pupils can write a fraction with a given numerator or denominator equivalent to one shown.

Oral questions

1. How many fifths in $2\frac{3}{5}$?
2. Write $\frac{13}{4}$ as a mixed number.
3. I am thinking of a fraction. It has 12 as its denominator and it is equivalent to $\frac{1}{3}$. What is the numerator?
4. Which two of these fractions are equivalent: $\frac{2}{3}, \frac{1}{2}, \frac{2}{6}, \frac{4}{6}$?

Common difficulties

Pupils may find it difficult to convert a mixed number to an improper fraction or vice versa. Provide images for pupils to help them with the conversion, e.g. for $\frac{13}{4}$, ask *How many quarters in one whole?* Then draw a shape and divide it into quarters. *How many quarters in two whole ones?* etc. Do the same with mixed numbers, e.g. to show $3\frac{1}{2}$ as an improper fraction draw three and a half circles, divide each whole into halves and count the halves.

Practice activities

1 Pick two cards – one from 2–5, one from 10–20. Write the larger number over the smaller number to form an improper fraction and convert it to a mixed number.

2 Draw two squares of the same size. Divide one in half and the other into an even number of equal parts. Shade in half of the second square and write down the equivalent fraction shown, e.g. if the shape is divided into eight equal parts, four of the eight parts should be shaded, showing that $\frac{4}{8} = \frac{1}{2}$. Repeat with other simple fractions, e.g. $\frac{1}{4}, \frac{3}{4}, \frac{1}{3}, \frac{2}{3}$ (for $\frac{1}{3}$ and $\frac{2}{3}$ the shapes will need to be divided into a number of parts divisible by 3).

Answers

1. 13 **2.** $3\frac{1}{4}$ **3.** 4 **4.** $\frac{2}{3}, \frac{4}{6}$

5. $4\frac{3}{4}$ **6.** $2\frac{2}{5}$ **7.** $3\frac{1}{3}$

8. join a to g, b to j, c to f, d to i, e to h

9a. $\frac{4}{6}, \frac{6}{9}, \frac{8}{12}$ **9b.** $\frac{10}{12}, \frac{15}{18}$ **9c.** $\frac{6}{8}, \frac{9}{12}$

Name ________________________________ **N7** **N8**

1. [ ] **2.** [ ] **3.** [ ] **4.** [ ]

/4

Write the mixed number represented by each picture.

5.

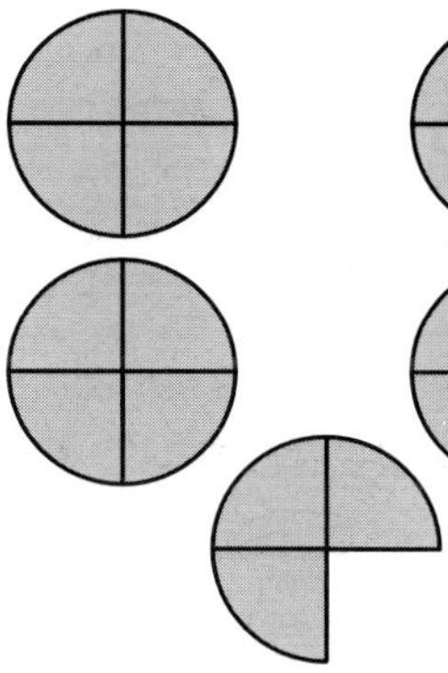

6.

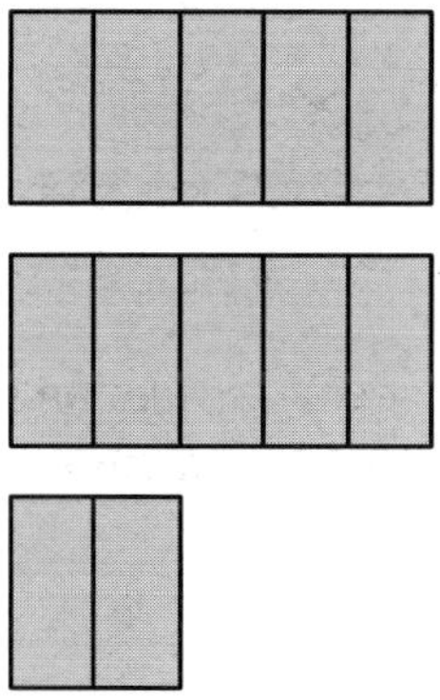

7.

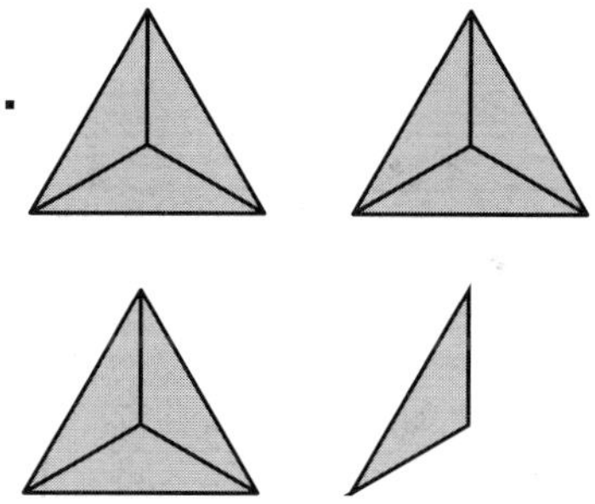

/3

8. Join each mixed number to the correct improper fraction.

a	$2\frac{1}{3}$	**f**	$\frac{15}{4}$
b	$3\frac{2}{3}$	**g**	$\frac{7}{3}$
c	$3\frac{3}{4}$	**h**	$\frac{17}{5}$
d	$4\frac{1}{4}$	**i**	$\frac{17}{4}$
e	$3\frac{2}{5}$	**j**	$\frac{11}{3}$

/5

9. Underline the fractions in each set that are equivalent to the fraction in the box.

a	$\boxed{\frac{2}{3}}$	$\frac{4}{6}$	$\frac{3}{9}$	$\frac{6}{9}$	$\frac{8}{12}$	$\frac{3}{6}$
b	$\boxed{\frac{5}{6}}$	$\frac{6}{12}$	$\frac{10}{12}$	$\frac{15}{18}$	$\frac{3}{12}$	$\frac{6}{8}$
c	$\boxed{\frac{3}{4}}$	$\frac{3}{5}$	$\frac{6}{9}$	$\frac{6}{8}$	$\frac{9}{12}$	$\frac{3}{8}$

/7

Score: [ ] /19 Total: [ ]

Fractions

Skills summary

- To find fractions of quantities
- To relate fractions to division
- To recognise simple relationships between fractions.

Diagnostic materials

Number Textbook 1, page 28, questions 1 to 10
- Check pupils can calculate unitary fraction amounts of quantities.

Number Textbook 1, page 29, questions 1 to 7
- Check pupils can use related fractions to find fractions of quantities.

Oral questions

1. Find $\frac{3}{5}$ of 15.
2. $\frac{1}{4}$ of a number is 8. What is the number?
3. $\frac{1}{2}$ of a number is 24. Calculate $\frac{1}{4}$ of the same number.
4. I know that $\frac{1}{6}$ of a number is 4. What is $\frac{1}{3}$ of the same number?

Common difficulties

Pupils can struggle when moving from finding unitary fraction amounts (e.g. $\frac{1}{3}$) to non-unitary fraction amounts (e.g. $\frac{2}{3}$). Provide images for them, e.g. to calculate $\frac{2}{3}$ of 15 encourage them to find $\frac{1}{3}$ of 15 by dividing cubes into three equal groups. Then emphasise that each group is $\frac{1}{3}$ of 15 – ask *So how would you make $\frac{2}{3}$ of 15?*

Use images of shapes that are the same divided into thirds and then sixths to demonstrate that $\frac{1}{6}$ is half of $\frac{1}{3}$. Divide counters or cubes equally between the parts of the shape, e.g. for 12 cubes place four in each third, and two in each sixth.

Practice activities

1 Write down the multiples of 12 from 12 to 48. Find $\frac{1}{2}$ of each and use the information to find $\frac{1}{4}$ of each. Repeat with $\frac{1}{3}$ of each and $\frac{1}{6}$ of each.

2 You need two sets of number cards: one set showing multiples of 10 from 20 to 100, the other showing the fractions $\frac{2}{5}$, $\frac{3}{5}$, $\frac{4}{5}$, $\frac{3}{10}$, $\frac{7}{10}$, $\frac{9}{10}$, $\frac{1}{10}$. Pick a card from each pile, write down the multiplication and work out the answer.

Answers

1. 9	**2.** 32	**3.** 12	**4.** 8
5. 2	**6.** 20	**7.** 2	**8.** 7
9. 10	**10.** 3	**11.** 3	**12.** 18

13. Output 1: 10 20 Output 2: 3 6 5 10
14. Output 1: 8 30 Output 2: 5 10 4 15

Name ____________________ **N9**

1. $\square$ **2.** $\square$ **3.** $\square$ **4.** $\square$

$\frac{\square}{4}$

Fill in the missing numbers so that each number sentence is correct.

5. $\frac{1}{\square}$ of 16 = 8 **6.** $\frac{1}{5}$ of $\square$ = 4 **7.** $\frac{\square}{3}$ of 12 = 8

8. $\frac{1}{\square}$ of 21 = 3 **9.** $\frac{2}{5}$ of $\square$ = 4 **10.** $\frac{\square}{8}$ of 24 = 9

11. $\frac{\square}{4}$ of 20 = 15 **12.** $\frac{1}{6}$ of $\square$ = 3

$\frac{\square}{8}$

Complete the tables showing the 'outputs' for each function machine.

13. The function machine finds $\frac{1}{2}$ of a number, then $\frac{1}{4}$ of the same number.

Input	8	12	24	20	40
Output 1	4	6	12		
Output 2	2				

14. The function machine finds $\frac{1}{3}$ of a number, then $\frac{1}{6}$ of the same number.

Input	12	30	60	24	90
Output 1	4	10	20		
Output 2	2				

$\frac{\square}{12}$

Score: $\square$ /24 Total: $\square$

Addition and subtraction

Skills summary

- To recognise what must be added to a 3-digit number to make the next multiple of 100
- To derive quickly addition pairs to 100 and 1000 (multiples of 10)
- To add several 1- and 2-digit numbers or numbers which are multiples of 10 or 100

Diagnostic materials

Number Textbook 1, page 31, questions 13 to 28
- Check pupils can calculate how much must be added to a 3-digit number to make the next multiple of 100.

Number Textbook 1, page 32, questions 1 to 15
- Check pupils can derive quickly pairs of multiples of 10 which make 1000 and record answers as subtractions.

Number Textbook 1, page 37, questions 1 to 10
- Check pupils can add several 2-digit amounts of money.

Oral questions

1. What must be added to 37 to make 100?
2. I am thinking of a number. I add 45 to it and get 100. What number did I start with?
3. Find the sum of 20, 80 and 63.
4. 80 and 70 are added. How much more needs to be added to make 200?

Common difficulties

When deriving pairs to 100 or 1000 it is common for pupils to mistakenly write the complement of, for example, 45 as 65, because 4 and 6 make 10, and 5 and 5 make 10. Encourage pupils to think about 'how many more' is needed to make the next ten or hundred, i.e. 5, then how many from the next ten or hundred to the next hundred or thousand, i.e. 50. Use a 100 square showing the numbers 1 to 100, or multiples of 10 in order to 1000, to provide an image.

Pupils can often be daunted by two or three multiples of 10 or 100. Make connections between addition of 1-digit numbers and 2-digit multiples of 10, e.g. *If you can add 3 and 6 and 7, you can add 30 and 60 and 70.* Similarly, link 2-digit numbers and 3-digit multiples of 10. Encourage pupils to find numbers that are easy to add, e.g. pairs that make 10 or 100, near doubles, etc.

Practice activities

1 Using place-value cards, pick a hundreds card and a tens card. Write down the number formed, e.g. if 200 and 80 are picked then write 280. Calculate how many more are needed to make 1000.

2 Pick three 2-digit number cards. Write down an addition sentence and find the total. Record the stages in your calculation.

Answers

1. 63 **2.** 55 **3.** 163 **4.** 50

6, 8, 10, 11 and 12 should be ticked

13. 63 **14.** 76 **15.** 130 **16.** 155 **17.** 7 **18.** 9 **19.** 5 **20.** 8

21. 42, 27, 51 **22.** 51, 49, 16 **23.** 16, 34, 27 **24.** 23, 34, 55

Name ______________________

N10 N11

1. [ ] 2. [ ] 3. [ ] 4. [ ]

/4

Tick the pairs that add to make 1000.

5. 650 450 [ ]

6. 320 680 [ ]

7. 270 630 [ ]

8. 560 440 [ ]

9. 110 990 [ ]

10. 230 770 [ ]

11. 150 850 [ ]

12. 340 660 [ ]

/8

Complete the calculations.

13. 37 + ____ = 100

14. 124 + ____ = 200

15. 300 – 170 = ____

16. 500 – ____ = 345

/4

Complete the calculations.

17. 5 + 6 + 4 + 5 + ____ = 27

18. 9 + 1 + 7 + 4 + ____ = 30

19. 6 + 6 + ____ + 7 + 8 = 32

20. 12 + ____ + 5 + 15 = 40

/4

Choose three numbers from the list to make each total.

23 38 42 27 51 49 16 34 55

21. 120 ______________

22. 116 ______________

23. 77 ______________

24. 112 ______________

/4

Score: [ ] /24 Total: [ ]

Adding 4-digit numbers

Skills summary

- To add 4-digit numbers using informal written methods
- To add 4-digit numbers using a standard written method
- To approximate an answer to a 4-digit addition

Diagnostic materials

Number Textbook 1, page 38, questions 1 to 14
- Check pupils can approximate and find the total of two 4-digit numbers

Number Textbook 1, page 40, questions 1 to 7
- Check pupils can approximate and find the total of three 4-digit numbers

Oral questions

1. Find the total of 4000, 6000 and 5000.
2. What is the sum of 6000, 8000 and 9000?
3. Find the total of 5600 and 3400.
4. Does the following pair of numbers give an answer of approximately 4000 or 3000: 2678 and 1329?

Common difficulties

When moving from the expanded method for addition to a standard written method it is important that pupils are aware that the calculation is the same but it is recorded in a slightly different way. Recording the two calculations alongside one another when explaining the contracted method will help develop pupils' understanding. Encourage pupils to emphasise the value of the digits when working through any calculation.

Practice activities

1 Pick four 1-digit number cards to form a 4-digit number. Rearrange the digits to make another number. Find the total. Rearrange the digits to find as many different totals as possible.

2 Form two 4-digit numbers using all the number cards 2–9. Find the total. Rearrange the number cards and find the totals again. Try to find all the possible totals.

Answers

1. 15 000 **2.** 23 000 **3.** 9000 **4.** 4000

7 and **8** should be ticked

9. 5993 **10.** 8021 **11.** 6226

12. 4574 + 2567 = 7141 **13.** 2836 + 6192 = 9028

14. 5728 + 3321 = 9049 **15.** 6465 + 8739 = 15 204

Name ______________________________

N12

1. [ ] **2.** [ ] **3.** [ ] **4.** [ ]

[ ] / 4

Tick the additions that would give an answer of approximately 5000.

5. 1352 + 2139 [ ]

6. 4012 + 3624 [ ]

7. 2017 + 2986 [ ]

8. 956 + 3963 [ ]

[ ] / 4

Complete these additions.

9. 3268 + 2725

10. 4113 + 3908

11. 2592 + 3634

[ ] / 3

Fill in the missing numbers.

12.

	4	[ ]	7	4
+	2	5	[ ]	7
	7	1	4	[ ]

13.

		[ ]	8	3	6
+		6	[ ]	9	2
		9	0	[ ]	8

14.

	5	7	2	[ ]
+	[ ]	3	2	1
	9	0	[ ]	9

15.

		6	[ ]	6	5
+		8	7	3	[ ]
	1	[ ]	2	0	4

[ ] / 4

Score: [ ] / 15 Total: [ ]

Number sequences

Skills summary

- To count on or back in steps of a constant size
- To construct number sequences
- To recognise patterns in number sequences
- To recognise multiples of numbers to the 10th multiple
- To begin to recognise common multiples

Diagnostic materials

Number Textbook 1, page 43, questions 1 to 12
- Check pupils can count on in steps of a constant size from numbers other than zero.

Number Textbook 1, page 44, questions 9 to 18
- Check pupils can identify common multiples using a multiplication square.

Oral questions

1. Write the next number in the sequence: 3, 23, 43, 63.
2. How much is being added on each time in this sequence: 7, 12, 17, 22?
3. Write the third multiple of six.
4. I am an even number between 20 and 40 and I am a multiple of 3 and 5. Which number am I?

Common difficulties

Pupils may struggle to recognise patterns in number sequences. When looking at sequences that increase or decrease in steps of a constant size encourage pupils to find the difference between two consecutive terms in the sequence to find the size of the step. Once they have found the pattern they can check it by adding it to another term.

To find common multiples pupils need to be able to recognise or derive quickly the multiples of each number. Practise counting up the multiples referring to a multiplication grid, then a counting stick with some of the multiples marked on, and then a counting stick with no numbers marked on.

Practice activities

1 Pick two number cards from 1–20. Choose one to be the starting number and the other to be the size of the step, e.g. if 7 and 12 are chosen, then 12 could be the starting number and 7 the size of the step. Write the first eight numbers in the sequence, i.e. 12, 19, 26, 33 etc. Repeat with two more cards.

2 Roll two ten-sided dice (if one or zero is rolled roll again). Write down two common multiples of the numbers rolled, e.g. if 4 and 6 are rolled you could write down 12, 24, etc.

Answers

1. 83 **2.** 5 **3.** 18 **4.** 30
5. 93, 113 **6.** 145, 95 **7.** 67,78 **8.** 310, 295
9. 15, 60, 30, 45, 90 should be circled
10. 15 **11.** 12 **12.** 21 **13.** 30 **14.** 40

Name ______________________ **N13** **N14**

1. [ ] **2.** [ ] **3.** [ ] **4.** [ ]

/4

Write the missing numbers in the sequences below.

5. 13, 33, 53, 73, ____, ____, 133

6. 220, 195, 170, ____, 120 ____, 70

7. 34, 45, 56, ____, ____, 89, 100

8. 340, 325, ____, ____, 280, 265, 250

/8

9. Circle the numbers that are multiples of 3 **and** 5.

6 15 21 25 60 23

30 16 35 45 90 53

/5

Join each sentence to a correct answer.

10. a multiple of 3 and 5.

11. a multiple of 4 and 3.

12. a multiple of 3 and 7.

13. a multiple of 2, 3, 5.

14. a multiple of 2, 4, 5.

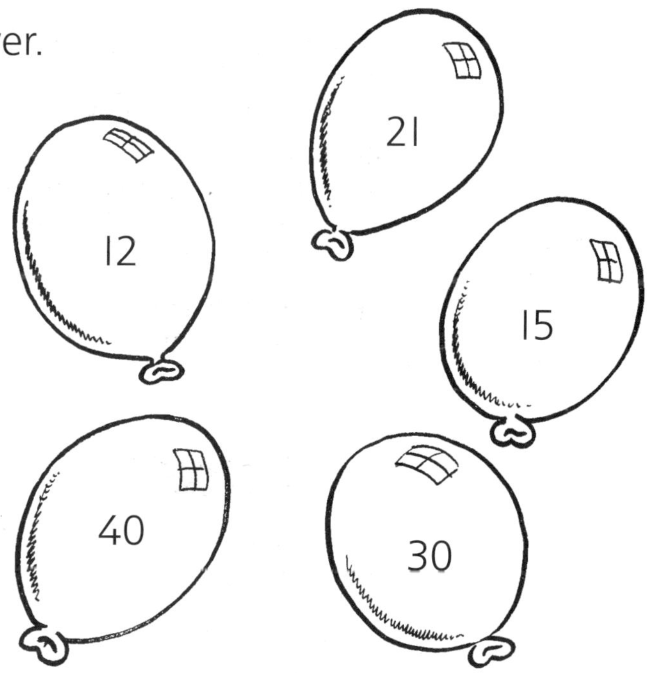

/5

Score: [ ] /22 Total: [ ]

Multiplication and division up to 10 000

Skills summary

- To multiply any positive integer up to 10 000 by 10 or 100
- To divide any positive integer up to 10 000 by 10 or 100
- To multiply a 2-digit multiple of 10 by a single digit number
- To multiply a 3-digit multiple of 100 by a single digit number

Diagnostic materials

Number Textbook 1, page 47, questions 14 to 21

- Check pupils are able to complete missing number problems using knowledge of multiplication by 10 or 100.

Number Textbook 1, page 57, questions 11 to 20

- Check pupils are able to use known multiplication facts to multiply a 3-digit multiple of 100 by a 1-digit number.

Oral questions

1. Multiply 304 by 100. Write the answer in words.
2. I am thinking of a number. I multiply it by 10 and the answer I get is 1800. What number did I start with?
3. What is 40 × 7?
4. Multiply 6 by 500.

Common difficulties

Avoid teaching pupils the trick of adding a zero or two zeros when multiplying by 10 or 100 or knocking zeros off when dividing. This can lead to confusion when pupils begin work with decimals when the 'trick' has to be untaught. Ask pupils to hold up number cards and move their position when multiplied by 10 one place to the left.

Encourage pupils to use what they know in order to multiply larger numbers, e.g. that to multiply 3 × 60 they can multiply 3 x 6 and then make the answer ten times bigger because 60 is 10 × 6. It is not helpful to learn tricks such as counting zeros in the question and zeros in the answer because this can lead to difficulties when doing calculations, such as 50 × 400 which = 20 000. Pupils counting zeros will commonly write 2000 as the answer.

Practice activities

1 Roll three ten-sided dice to form a 3-digit number. Multiply the number formed by 100. Write down the answer. Repeat ten times. Look at the numbers written down and divide each one by 100.

2 Pick two place-value cards – a ten card and a hundred card – and multiply the two numbers together. Write down the calculation and the answer.

Answers

1. Thirty thousand, four hundred **2.** 180 **3.** 280 **4.** 3000
5. 20 × 60, 300 × 4 **6.** 5 × 300, 15 × 100, 30 x 50 **7.** 40 × 50
8. 50 × 60, 10 × 300 **9.** 10 **10.** 305 **11.** 217
12. 45 600 **13.** 2340 **14.** 100 **15.** 10 **16.** 540 000

Name ______________________________

N15 N18 N19

1. ______________________________________

2. [ ] 3. [ ] 4. [ ]

/4

Underline the multiplications that will give the answer in the box.

5.	1200	20 × 60	300 × 4	30 × 4	2 × 6000
6.	1500	5 × 300	15 × 10	15 × 100	30 × 50
7.	2000	400 × 50	40 × 50	20 × 10	2 × 100
8.	3000	50 × 600	500 × 60	50 × 60	10 × 300

/8

Complete each of the calculations below.

9. 25 × ____ = 250

10. ____ × 100 = 30500

11. ____ × 10 = 2170

12. 456 × 100 = ____

13. ____ ÷ 10 = 234

14. 6700 ÷ ____ = 67

15. 4100 ÷ ____ = 410

16. ____ ÷ 100 = 5400

/8

Score: [ ] /20 Total: [ ]

Doubling and halving

Skills summary

- To use doubling and halving to help multiply and divide
- To derive multiplication facts by doubling or halving known facts
- To multiply two numbers by halving one and doubling the other
- To multiply by 5 (or 50), by multiplying by 10 (or 100), then halving
- To multiply by 25, using the fact that 4 × 25 = 100

Diagnostic materials

Number Textbook 1, page 52, questions 1 to 9
- Check pupils can use doubling and halving to multiply.

Number Textbook 1, page 56, questions 1 to 9
- Check pupils can multiply numbers by 50 and 25, starting by multiplying by 100.

Number Textbook 1, page 63, questions 1 to 9
- Check pupils can divide by 4 by halving and halving again.

Oral questions

1. I know 7 lots of 8 is 56. So what are 14 lots of 8?
2. What is 50 × 38?
3. Divide 148 by 4.
4. If 112 sweets are shared between 8 friends, how many do they each get?

Common difficulties

Pupils will find it difficult applying their knowledge of doubles and halves to a range of calculations if they are not confident with doubling and halving. Provide lots of opportunities for them to double and halve and encourage pupils to partition numbers in order to make doubling or halving easier, i.e. double or halve each part and then recombine. Provide pupils with images so that they can see that ÷4 = ÷2÷2 etc.

Practice activities

1 Pick two cards from a selection of multiples of 4 from 4 to 48. Multiply the two numbers by doubling one number and halving the other, e.g. *8 × 20 = 4 × 40 = 2 × 80 = 160*. Write down each stage of the calculation.

2 Form a 2-digit number by choosing two place-value cards – a tens and a units card. Write down the number generated and multiply it by 100, then 50 then 25.

Answers

1. 112 **2.** 1900 **3.** 37 **4.** 14
5. join a to g, b to f, c to h, d to e
6. first row: 4200, 3600, 3500, 5300; second row: 2100, 1800, 1750, 2650
7, **10** and **11** should be ticked

Name ______________________________ **N16** **N17** **N20**

1. ☐ **2.** ☐ **3.** ☐ **4.** ☐

☐ /4

5. Use knowledge of doubling and halving to join calculations that are equivalent.

a 16 × 23

b 24 × 13

c 12 × 37

d 9 × 54

e 18 × 27

f 6 × 52

g 8 × 46

h 3 × 148

☐ /4

6. Complete the table below.

×	24	42	36	35	53
100	2400				
50	1200				

☐ /8

Tick the calculations below that are correct.

7. 68 ÷ 4 = 17 ☐

8. 128 ÷ 8 = 18 ☐

9. 212 ÷ 4 = 54 ☐

10. 96 ÷ 6 = 16 ☐

11. 248 ÷ 8 = 31 ☐

12. 306 ÷ 6 = 50 ☐

☐ /6

Score: ☐ /22 Total: ☐

Tenths and hundredths

Skills summary

- To recognise decimal notation for tenths and hundredths
- To know the value of each digit in a 2-place decimal number
- To order a set of decimal numbers
- To recognise the equivalence between decimals and fractions

Diagnostic materials

Number Textbook 1, page 68, top

- Check pupils are able to order a set of decimal numbers, including 1- and 2-place decimals.

Number Textbook 1, page 70, questions 1 to 13

- Check pupils are able to add and subtract simple fractions to and from decimal numbers.

Oral questions

1. (Write 2·73 on the board.) What is the seven worth in this number?
2. Listen to these numbers: 2·6, 2·45, 2·3. Write down the largest.
3. Write $1\frac{3}{10}$ as a decimal.
4. What is 4·75 as a mixed number?

Common difficulties

Pupils struggle with ordering a mixture of 1- and 2-place decimals. They tend to think that a 2-place decimal is larger than a 1-place decimal, e.g. 2·35 is larger than 2·4. Use base 10 apparatus (with the hundred block as a whole one, tens rods as tenths, and units blocks as hundredths) to provide an image for pupils so that they can see that 2·4 is the same as 2·40.

When converting fractions to decimals pupils often think the numbers in both must be the same, hence $\frac{1}{10}$ as a fraction becomes 1·10. Draw pictures to represent given fractions and decimals so they can see that 1·10 cannot be a sensible answer.

Practice activities

1. Roll a ten-sided dice three times. Write the 2-place decimal number rolled. Repeat until 10 numbers have been generated. Write them in order from smallest to largest.
2. Pick two digit cards to form a 1-place decimal number. Write down the number as a decimal and then as a fraction.

Answers

1. $\frac{7}{10}$ or 7 tenths **2.** 2·6 **3.** 1·3 **4.** $4\frac{3}{4}$ or $4\frac{75}{100}$
5. 1, 0·6 and 0·05 should be circled **6.** 2, 0·3, 0·08 should be circled
7. 0·5, 0·07 should be circled **8.** 3, 0·04 should be circled
9. 1·6, 1·85, 2·25, 2·5, 2·75, 2·8
10. from left to right 1·25, $1\frac{1}{2}$, $1\frac{7}{10}$, 1·9

Name ______________________________

N21 N22

I. [ ] 2. [ ] 3. [ ] 4. [ ]

/4

Circle the numbers in each set that add to make the number in the box.

5. [1·65] 0·01 0·5 I 6 0·05 0·1 5 0·6 0·06

6. [2·38] 8 0·03 0·8 0·3 2 3 0·2 0·02 0·08

7. [0·57] 5 0·5 0·7 7 0·07 0·05

8. [3·04] 3 0·4 0·3 4 0·04 0·03

/4

9. Write these decimals in order.

2·25 1·6 2·8 2·5 1·85 2·75

[ ] [ ] [ ] [ ] [ ] [ ]

smallest

largest

/6

10. Complete the missing numbers on the number line.

Decimals

1	[ ]	1·5	1·7	[ ]	2
1	$1\frac{1}{4}$	[ ]	[ ]	$1\frac{9}{10}$	2

Fractions

/4

Score: [ ] /18 Total: [ ]

Hundreds, tens and units

Skills summary

- To add HTU and TU by partitioning
- To subtract TU from HTU by partitioning
- To add or subtract 3-digit near multiples of 10 and 100 to or from a 3-digit number
- To find a difference by counting up from a smaller number to a larger one

Diagnostic materials

Number Textbook 2, page 3, questions 1 to 10
- Check pupils can add a multiple of 10 to a 3-digit number.

Number Textbook 2, page 8, questions 1 to 8
- Check pupils can subtract a near multiple of 100 from a 3-digit number.

Number Textbook 2, page 11, questions 1 to 7
- Check pupils can find the difference between a multiple of 1000 and a 4-digit number.

Oral questions

1. What is 34 more than 127?
2. Subtract 43 from 152.
3. How much more than 197 is 338?
4. Find the difference between 3014 and 2997.

Common difficulties

When using partitioning as a strategy to add or subtract numbers pupils often struggle to hold all the different 'parts' in their head. Encourage pupils to jot down parts of the calculation as they go, e.g. to calculate 156 + 78 jot down 150 + 70 = 220, 6 + 8 = 14, 220 + 14 = 234. This also helps develop their mechanisms of recording so that they can explain a mental strategy to someone else.

To count up from smaller numbers to larger ones pupils need to remember to tackle this in stages. Use the 'zigzag' method (or complementary addition) to provide a structure.

Practice activities

1 Form a 2-digit number and a 3-digit number using place-value cards. Partition the numbers and recombine to find the total. Record the stages of the calculation. Repeat, this time forming a subtraction question.

2 Write down 7000. Roll a six-sided dice four times and form the largest possible 4-digit number. Subtract the number from 7000 by counting up from the smaller to the larger number. How many jumps are needed?

Answers

1. 161	**2.** 109	**3.** 141	**4.** 17
5. 208	**6.** 273	**7.** 218	**8.** 295
9. 316 – 97	**10.** 352 + 97	**11.** 387 + 198	**12.** 378 + 97
13. 317 – 198	**14.** 354 – 198	**15, 16, 18** and **20** should be ticked	

Name ______________________________ N23 N24 N25

1. ☐ 2. ☐ 3. ☐ 4. ☐

/4

Complete these calculations.

5. 142 + 66 = ____

6. 225 + 48 = ____

7. 262 − 44 = ____

8. 357 − 62 = ____

/4

Choose numbers from the list to make each calculation correct.
A number may be used more than once.

354 316 387 352 317 378 97 198

9. ____ − ____ = 219

10. ____ + ____ = 449

11. ____ + ____ = 585

12. ____ + ____ = 475

13. ____ − ____ = 119

14. ____ − ____ = 156

/6

Tick the subtractions that have a difference of 17.

15. 304 − 287 ☐

16. 3004 − 2987 ☐

17. 506 − 499 ☐

18. 516 − 499 ☐

19. 4008 − 3997 ☐

20. 4008 − 3991 ☐

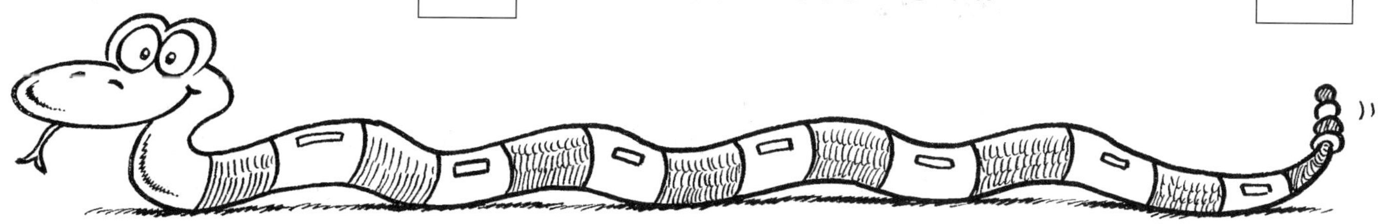

/6

Score: ☐ /20 Total: ☐

Subtraction

Skills summary

- To subtract by taking away or finding the difference
- To choose the most appropriate strategy for subtraction
- To subtract HTU from ThHTU using a standard written method

Diagnostic materials

Number Textbook 2, page 14, questions 1 to 7
- Check pupils are able to set out a subtraction correctly and subtract a 3-digit number from a 4-digit number using a standard written method.

Number Textbook 2, page 16
- Check pupils are able to carry out subtractions using the suggested strategy.

Number Textbook 2, page 19
- Check pupils can complete subtraction word problems using appropriate strategies.

Oral questions

1. Subtract 2500 from 4300.
2. How much more than 760 is 1280?
3. Find the difference between 2300 and 1997.
4. What is left if 125 is taken away from 4500?

Common difficulties

It is important that pupils are taught the range of subtraction strategies available to them so that they can make an informed choice. Encourage pupils to read the calculation carefully before deciding upon the strategy to use and to jot down the steps needed to help them complete the calculation.

Demonstrate decomposition using Base 10 equipment. Talk through the procedure, perhaps by showing the expanded version, asking pupils to explain the procedure in their own words. Pupils may become confused if a calculation is not written down, especially when the two numbers have a different number of digits. Show how the calculation cannot work if numbers are put in the wrong columns.

Practice activities

1 Roll a ten-sided dice three times to generate a 3-digit number. Repeat to make six numbers. Use the numbers rolled to make three subtractions. Make one that can be completed by taking away, one by counting up, and one by rounding. If necessary rearrange the digits. (Not all the 3-digit numbers generated need to be used.)

2 Use a ten-sided dice to generate three 4-digit numbers and three 3-digit numbers. Find the difference between each 4-digit number and each 3-digit number. How many different calculations can be made?

Answers

1. 1800 **2.** 520 **3.** 303 **4.** 4375

5. 229 **6.** 213 **7.** 11 **8.** 1223 **9.** 2248 **10.** 33

11. 2612 – 841 = 1771 **12.** 3248 – 783 = 2465 **13.** 4325 – 267 = 4058

Check that an appropriate strategy has been chosen in each case.

Name ____________________

N26 N27

1. □ **2.** □ **3.** □ **4.** □

□ / 4

Write the calculations in the appropriate box according to how best to solve them. Then complete the calculations. The first one has been done for you.

5. 328 – 99 **6.** 256 – 43 **7.** 307 – 296

8. 1288 – 65 **9.** 2447 – 199 **10.** 2013 – 1980

Taking away	Rounding	Counting on
	5. 328 – 99 = 229	

□ / 5

Write in the missing numbers.

11.

□	6	□	2
–	8	4	□
1	□	7	1

12.

3	□	4	8
–	7	□	□
□	4	6	5

13.

□	3	2	□	
–	□	6	7	
4	0	□	8	

□ / 3

Score: □ /12 Total: □

Factors

Skills summary

- To apply divisibility tests for 2, 4, 5, 10 or 100
- To recognise factor pairs for numbers up to 100

Diagnostic materials

Number Textbook 2, page 22, questions 1 to 15

- Check pupils can use divisibility to test which numbers are divisible by 2, 4, 5 or 10.

Number Textbook 2, page 23, questions 1 to 10

- Check pupils are able to use multiplication facts to find factors of given numbers.

Oral questions

1. Is 428 divisible by 4?
2. Write a number less than 100 which is divisible by 2, 4, 5 and 10.
3. Listen to these numbers: 2, 3, 4, 5. Which is not a factor of 12?
4. Write down a pair of factors for the number 35, not including 1 and 35.

Common difficulties

Pupils can become confused when looking for numbers divisible by 4 as other divisibility rules require them to look at the last digit. Encourage them first to see if the last digit is even and then to divide by 2, using partitioning to help make the halving easier. Some pupils might find it useful to know that if the last two digits in any number are divisible by 4 then the whole number is divisible by 4.

In order to find factors of numbers quickly, pupils need a secure grasp of multiplication facts. Pupils who are less secure with their tables facts would benefit from using a multiplication square for finding factors, although it is important to remember that they will not find *all* the factors, only the factors up to 10 or 12 (depending on the size of the square).

Practice activities

1 Write the numbers 2, 4, 5 and 10 down the left-hand side of the page. Generate a 3-digit number using a dice. Write the number formed next to any number in the list that it is divisible by. If it is not divisible by any of the numbers, write it on the right-hand side of the page. Continue until three numbers are written next to each number in the left-hand list.

2 Pick five cards from a set of 2-digit number cards. Write down all the factors for each of the numbers chosen.

Answers

1. yes	**2.** 20, 40, 60 or 80	**3.** 5	**4.** 5, 7
5. circle 378, 496	**6.** circle 412, 648	**7.** circle 450, 315	**8.** circle 310, 560
9. circle 3100, 5700		**10.** 12,18 and 24 should be ticked	
11. 24,12 and 36 should be ticked		**12.** 15, 45 and 30 should be ticked	

Name ______________________________

N28 N29

1. [ ] **2.** [ ] **3.** [ ] **4.** [ ]

/4

Circle the correct numbers in each list.

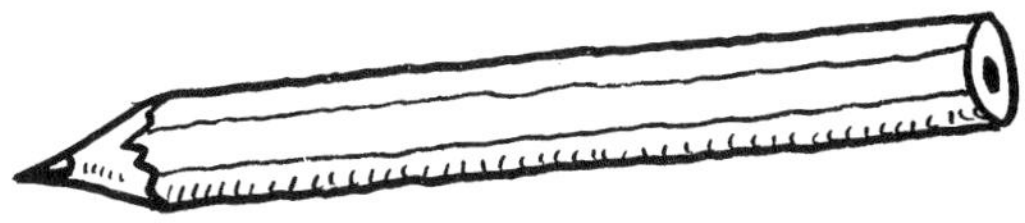

5.	Divisible by 2	23	245	378	496
6.	Divisible by 4	412	514	648	446
7.	Divisible by 5	553	450	315	203
8.	Divisible by 10	310	560	607	108
9.	Divisible by 100	1010	2007	3100	5700

/10

---

10. Tick the numbers that have 2 and 3 as factors.

12 [ ] 21 [ ] 15 [ ] 18 [ ] 24 [ ] 27 [ ]

11. Tick the numbers that have 3 and 4 as factors.

16 [ ] 18 [ ] 24 [ ] 12 [ ] 27 [ ] 36 [ ]

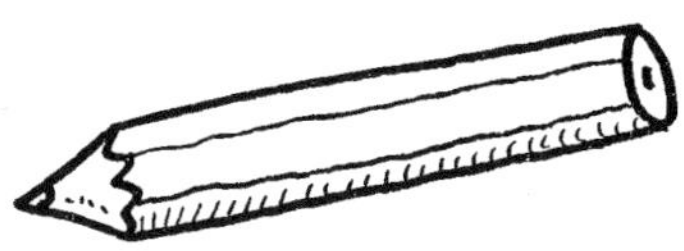

12. Tick the numbers that have 3 and 5 as factors.

25 [ ] 15 [ ] 45 [ ] 18 [ ] 40 [ ] 30 [ ]

/9

Score: [ ] /23 Total: [ ]

Positive and negative numbers

Skills summary

- To count back below zero
- To order a set of positive and negative numbers
- To understand how temperature will change after a given rise or fall

Diagnostic materials

Number Textbook 2, page 26, questions 1 and 2

- Check pupils are able to recognise numbers represented by positions on a number line.

Number Textbook 2, page 28, questions 1 to 10

- Check pupils are able to calculate the new temperature after a given rise or fall.

Oral questions

1. (Draw a number line on the board from ⁻10 to 10, mark on ⁻10, 0 and 10, draw an arrow to where ⁻6 would be.) Which number is indicated by the arrow?
2. Write down the largest number: 3, ⁻2, ⁻7, 1.
3. It is 5 °C. The temperature falls by 6 °C. What is the new temperature?
4. If a temperature of ⁻3 °C rises by 5 °C, what is the new temperature?

Common difficulties

When working with negative numbers, pupils can find it difficult to realise that ⁻5 is less than ⁻1 as 5 is more than 1. It is important to provide pupils with a number line that they can count along. Some pupils can be confused when the change is made from or to a vertical number line from or to a horizontal one. Show pupils it is the same thing by changing a vertical line to a horizontal one or vice versa to make the connection explicit.

Practice activities

1 Pick six cards from ⁻10 to 10. Draw a number line and mark the numbers chosen on the number line.

2 Roll two ten-sided dice (one red, one blue) twice each. Numbers on the red dice indicate negative numbers, numbers on the blue positive numbers. Write the numbers rolled in order.

Answers

1. ⁻6 **2.** 3 **3.** ⁻1 °C **4.** 2 °C
5. ⁻2 °C **6.** 0 °C **7.** ⁻8 °C **8.** ⁻3 °C
9. ⁻10, ⁻6, ⁻4, ⁻2, 0, 1, 3, 5
11. increase of 10 °C **12.** decrease of 5 °C **13.** decrease of 9 °C
14. increase of 4 °C

Name ____________________

1. [ ] **2.** [ ] **3.** [ ] **4.** [ ]

/4

Write the temperature shown on each thermometer.

5.

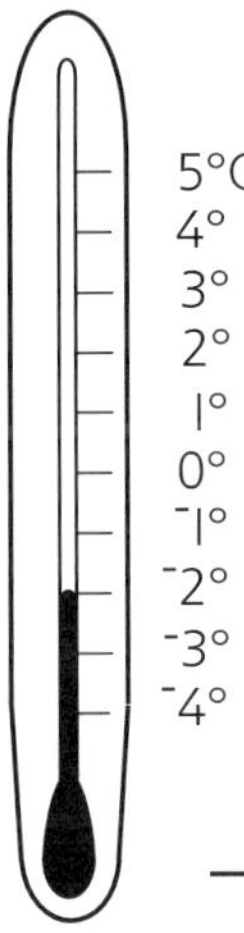

_____ °C

6.

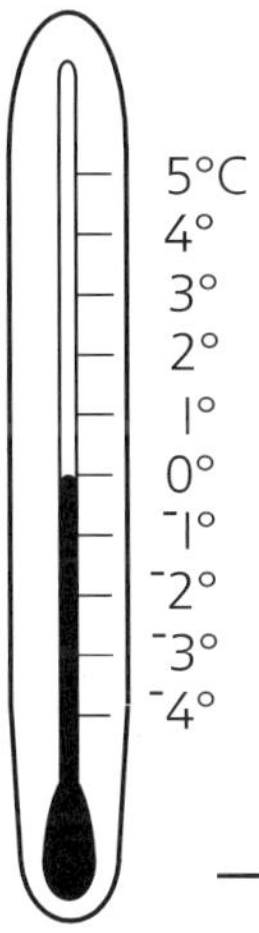

_____ °C

7.

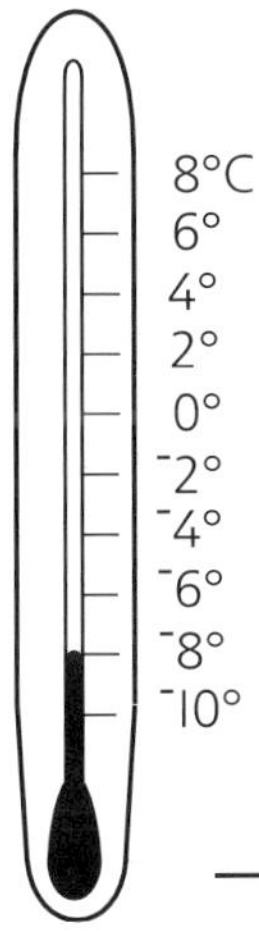

_____ °C

8.

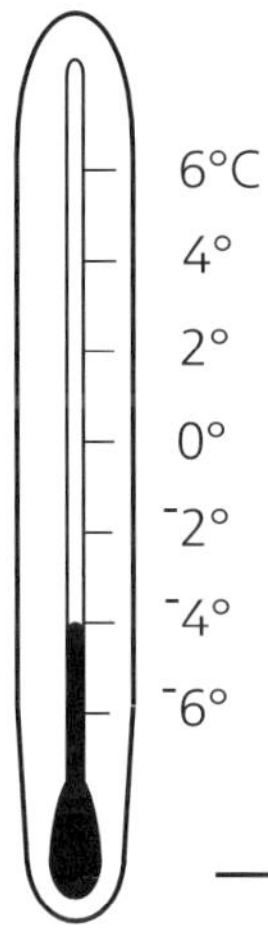

_____ °C

/4

9. Write these numbers in order.

$^{-}4$ 3 $^{-}2$ 0 5 $^{-}6$ 1 $^{-}10$

[ ] [ ] [ ] [ ] [ ] [ ] [ ] [ ]

smallest ... largest

/8

How much have the temperatures increased or decreased?

10. $^{-}2$ °C to $^{+}5$ °C *increase of 7 °C*

11. $^{-}3$ °C to $^{+}7$ °C ____________

12. $^{+}4$ °C to $^{-}1$ °C ____________

13. $^{+}5$ °C to $^{-}4$ °C ____________

14. $^{-}7$ °C to $^{-}3$ °C ____________

/4

Score: [ ] /20 Total: [ ]

Multiplication

Skills summary

- To multiply HTU × U using informal written methods
- To multiply HTU × U, and TU × TU using a standard written method
- To multiply U·t × U using a standard written method

Diagnostic materials

Number Textbook 2, page 29, questions 11 to 20
- Check pupils are able to use a standard expanded method to multiply HTU × U.

Number Textbook 2, page 31, questions 12 to 20
- Check pupils are able to use a standard expanded method to multiply TU × TU.

Oral questions

1. What is 320 multiplied by 3?
2. What is the product of 107 and 5?
3. Find 20 lots of 34.
4. Find the total length of four pieces of wood each 3·5 m long.

Common difficulties

Pupils may find it difficult to move from the informal written method (the grid layout) to the expanded standard method if they are not clear that it is the same calculation, just a different layout. It is important that the link between the two layouts is made. Encourage pupils to use facts that they know when multiplying larger numbers, e.g. to multiply 40 by 60, use 4 × 6 but remind them that the 40 is 10 times bigger than 4 so the answer will be 10 times bigger, and that 60 is 10 times bigger than 6 so the answer will be 10 times bigger again.

Practice activities

1 Use place-value cards to make a 3-digit number. Then pick a single digit card to multiply it by. Write down the multiplication. Use either an informal or a standard method to calculate the answer.

2 Pick four 2-digit numbers from a set of cards. Multiply each one by each of the others. How many different products can be made?

Answers

1. 960 **2.** 535 **3.** 680 **4.** 14 m
5. 60, 36, 1896 **6.** 80, 32, 1712 **7.** 1600, 480, 32, 2112
8. 2100, 280, 49, 2429 **9.** should be ticked
12. 25·8 **13.** 15·6 **14.** 18·9 **15.** 32

Name ____________________ **N31** **N32**

1. ☐ **2.** ☐ **3.** ☐ **4.** ☐

☐ /4

Complete the calculations below. Use the rectangles to help you.

5. 316 × 6 = ☐

	300	10	6
6	1800		

6. 428 × 4 = ☐

	400	20	8
4	1600		

7. 264 × 8 = ☐

	200	60	4
8			

8. 347 × 7 = ☐

	300	40	7
7			

☐ /4

Tick the calculations that are correct.

9.
```
   34
 × 23
   12
   90
   80
  600
  782
```
☐

10.
```
   26
 × 17
   42
   14
   60
  200
  316
```
☐

11.
```
   43
 × 24
   12
  160
   60
   80
  312
```
☐

☐ /3

Complete these calculations.

12. 4·3 × 6 = ☐

13. 5·2 × 3 = ☐

14. 2·7 × 7 = ☐

15. 6·4 × 5 = ☐

☐ /4

Score: ☐ /15 Total: ☐

Division

Skills summary

- To use the concept of a remainder
- To divide HTU or TU by U using informal written methods
- To divide HTU or TU by U using standard written methods

Diagnostic materials

Number Textbook 2, page 37, questions 10 to 18

- Check pupils are able to use an informal written method to divide a 3-digit number by a 1-digit number.

Number Textbook 2, page 41, questions 9 to 16

- Check pupils are able to use a standard written method to divide a 3-digit number by a 1-digit number and round their answer if necessary.

Oral questions

1. How many 3s in 42?
2. How much is left over once 53 is divided by 4?
3. What is 126 divided by 6?
4 Divide 225 by 5.

Common difficulties

To help pupils understand the written method for division it is important that they understand division as grouping or repeated subtraction. Pupils may find it difficult to hold all the facts they need in their head, so it is useful to encourage them to jot down useful multiples of the divisor, e.g. to calculate 324 ÷ 7 they should jot down 10 × 7 = 70, 20 × 7 = 140 etc.

Practice activities

1 Pick a 2-digit number card (from 10–99), and roll a dice to generate a divisor. Divide the 2-digit number by the number rolled. Write down the calculation. Score a point for each calculation that doesn't leave a remainder. Continue until three points have been scored.

2 Generate a 3-digit number using place-value cards then select a 1-digit card. Divide the 3-digit number by the 1-digit number. Write down and carry out the calculation.

Answers

1. 14 **2.** 1 **3.** 21 **4.** 45
5. a, d, e, g should be circled
6. 14 **7.** 24 r 1 **8.** 21 r 3 **9.** 14 r 2
10. 3 **11.** 4 **12.** 6

Name ________________________ **N33** **N34**

1. ☐ **2.** ☐ **3.** ☐ **4.** ☐

/4

5. Circle the calculations that give a remainder of 3.

a	27 ÷ 4	**b**	34 ÷ 2	**c**	39 ÷ 8	**d**	43 ÷ 4
e	35 ÷ 8	**f**	47 ÷ 6	**g**	45 ÷ 7	**h**	51 ÷ 3

/8

Complete these calculations.

6. 56 ÷ 4 =

7. 73 ÷ 3 =

8. 87 ÷ 4 =

9. 86 ÷ 6 =

/4

Write in the missing numbers.

10. ☐) 81, answer 27

11. ☐) 164, answer 41

12. ☐) 192, answer 32

/3

Score: ☐ /19 Total: ☐

Decimals

Skills summary

- To round a 1- or 2-place decimal to the nearest whole number
- To add mentally two decimal numbers with the same number of decimal places
- To subtract mentally one decimal number from another, where both numbers have the same number of decimal places

Diagnostic materials

Number Textbook 2, page 43, questions 1 to 3
- Check pupils can recognise the position of decimal numbers on a number line.

Number Textbook 2, page 47, questions 1 to 7
- Check pupils can add two 1-place decimal numbers.

Oral questions

1. Round 1·6 to the nearest whole number.
2. What is the nearest whole number to 2·49?
3. Find the total of 2·3 and 4·9.
4. Subtract 4·6 from 6·1.

Common difficulties

When working with 2-place decimal numbers it is common to think that, for example, 2·34 is larger than 2·5. Pupils need lots of work with number lines and apparatus, e.g. money or base 10 apparatus, to understand the value of tenths and hundredths. There can be confusion when rounding a 2-place decimal number to a whole number if the pupils first round it to the nearest tenth, e.g. 2·48 rounded to the nearest tenth is 2·5, which might then be rounded to 3. Ensure that pupils are encouraged to think about the value of the number and its position relative to other numbers.

When adding decimal numbers pupils need to know what happens when they bridge a unit (get ten tenths) to avoid 2·5 + 2·7 = 4·12. Pupils need to understand the value of each digit and not see the digits after the decimal point as separate from the rest of the number.

Practice activities

1 Pick three digit cards, one for the whole number, one for tenths, one for hundredths. Write down the number and its nearest whole number.

2 Roll two dice to generate a 1-place decimal number, e.g. 5·3. Repeat. Add the two numbers generated together, writing down the calculation. Using the same numbers find the difference between them.

Answers

1. 2 **2.** 2 **3.** 7·2 **4.** 1·5
5. 6·23 and 4·08 **6.** 1·77 and 2·89 **7.** 1·77 and 4·08 **8.** 6·23 and 2·89
9. join 2·7 and 2·6, 1·2 and 4·1, 4·8 and 0·5, 3·0 and 2·3, 3·9 and 1·4
10. 1·3 **11.** 0·22 **12.** 8·1 **13.** 3·16
14. 5·12 **15.** 5·39

Name ____________________ N35 N36

1. [ ] 2. [ ] 3. [ ] 4. [ ]

/4

Choose two numbers from the box that, when added together, give approximately the numbers below.

1·77 2·89 4·08 4·68 6·23

5. 10 ←

6. 5 ←

7. 6 ←

8. 9 ←

/4

9. Join pairs of numbers that total 5·3.

2·7 1·2 4·8 3·0 3·9

0·5 2·6 2·3 1·4 4·1

/5

Complete these calculations.

10. 3·6 – ____ = 2·3

11. 2·37 – 2·15 = ____

12. ____ – 3·4 = 4·7

13. 6·42 – 3·26 = ____

14. 7·53 – ____ = 2·41

15. ____ – 2·13 = 3·26

/6

Score: ____ /19 Total: ____

Fractions and percentages

Skills summary

- To express simple fractions as percentages
- To express percentages as fractions out of 100
- To recognise simple percentages of square grids
- To find simple percentages of quantities

Diagnostic materials

Number Textbook 2, page 52, questions 1 to 10
- Check pupils are able to recognise how much of a given shape has been shaded.

Number Textbook 2, page 53, questions 1 to 12
- Check pupils are able to find 50% of given quantities.

Oral questions

1. Write $\frac{3}{10}$ as a percentage.
2. What is 75% as a fraction?
3. Find 50% of £200.
4. What is 10% of £150?

Common difficulties

In order to work confidently with percentages pupils need to be clear about the relationship between fractions and percentages. It is important to stress that when converting a fraction to a percentage the fraction must first be written out of 100. Using a blank 100 square can provide an useful image: use shading to show that $\frac{1}{4}$ is 25 out of 100 squares.

Using a washing line, position fractions and percentages so that pupils can see which fractions/percentages are equivalent.

Practice activities

1 From a selection of 2-digit number cards (multiples of 5) choose eight cards. Each card shows a percentage. Write the percentage down and the fraction it is equivalent to.

2 Pick three hundreds place-value cards and three tens place-value cards to form three 3-digit multiples of 10. For each of the numbers calculate 50%, 10% and 20%.

Answers

1. 30% **2.** $\frac{3}{4}$ **3.** £100 **4.** £15
5. reading from left to right: $\frac{2}{10}$ or $\frac{1}{5}$, 25%, $\frac{1}{2}$ or $\frac{5}{10}$, 70%, $\frac{3}{4}$ or $\frac{75}{100}$
6. 70% **7.** 75% **8.** 40%
9. 30 **10.** 10% **11.** 50 **12.** 50% **13.** 34 **14.** 250

Name ______________________

N37

1. [ ] **2.** [ ] **3.** [ ] **4.** [ ]

/4

5. Complete the table of fraction and percentage equivalents.

Fraction	$\frac{1}{10}$		$\frac{1}{4}$		$\frac{7}{10}$	
Percentage	10%	20%		50%		75%

/5

Write the percentage of each shape that is **not** shaded.

6.

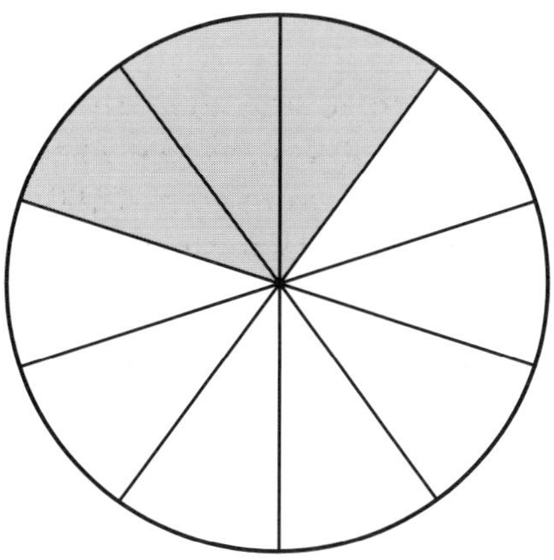

________%

7.

________%

8.

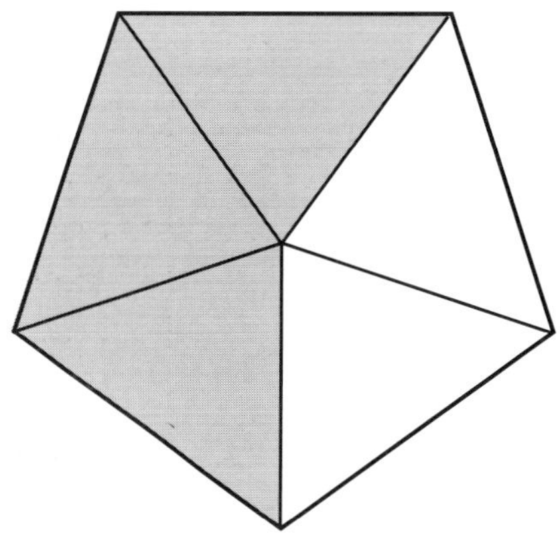

________%

/3

Complete the number sentences below.

9. 50% of 60 = ____

10. _____% of 200 = 20

11. 20% of ____ = 10

12. _____% of 32 = 16

13. 10% of 340 = ____

14. 10% of ____ = 25

/6

Score: [ ] /18 Total: [ ]

Decimals

Skills summary

- To approximate an answer to an addition involving two or more decimal numbers
- To derive quickly 1-place decimal addition pairs to 1 and 10
- To add two or more decimal numbers using standard written methods

Diagnostic materials

Number Textbook 2, page 56, questions 1 to 10
- Check pupils can use knowledge of deriving pairs of decimals that make 10 to find change from £10.

Number Textbook 2, page 59, questions 1 to 7
- Check pupils can approximate and find the total of three 2-place decimal numbers.

Oral questions

1. 10 subtract 4·3 leaves how many?
2. What is 2·25 more than 1·25?
3. I had £10. I spent £4.35. How much change do I have?
4. What is the total of 3·18, 5·86, and 4·93 to the nearest whole number?

Common difficulties

When deriving pairs to 1 or 10 it is common for pupils to mistakenly write the complement of, for example, 4·5 as 6·5, because 4 and 6 make 10, and 0·5 and 0·5 make 1. Encourage pupils to think about 'how many more' are needed to make the next whole one, i.e. 0·5, then how many from the next whole one to the next ten, i.e. 5. Use a hundred square showing 1-place decimals 0·1 to 10·0 to provide an image.

Practice activities

1. Pick two 1-digit cards, one to represent units and one to represent tenths. Work out how many more needs to be added to make 10. Write the answer as a subtraction.

2. Take a page from a newspaper or catalogue that shows prices. Choose three items and find the total cost.

Answers

1. 5·7 **2.** 3·5 **3.** £5.65 **4.** 14
5. join 4·6 to 5·4, 3·8 to 6·2, 2·5 to 7·5, 3·6 to 6·4, 4·2 to 5·8, 3·5 to 6·5
6. 6·15 **7.** 7·04 **8.** 8·80 **9.** 3·86 + 2·42 = 6·28
10. 5·17 + 2·84 = 8·01 **11.** 6·47 + 2·76 = 9·23

Name ____________________ **N38** **N39**

1. ☐ **2.** ☐ **3.** ☐ **4.** ☐

☐ /4

5. Join pairs that total 10.

4·6 3·8 2·5 3·6 4·2 3·5

6·2 6·4 7·5 6·5 5·4 5·8

☐ /6

Complete these additions.

6.
```
   3·21
 + 2·94
 ------
```

7.
```
   4·72
 + 2·32
 ------
```

8.
```
   5·61
 + 3·19
 ------
```

☐ /3

Fill in the missing numbers.

9.
```
   3 · ☐ 6
 + ☐ · 4 2
 ---------
   6 · 2 ☐
```

10.
```
   ☐ · 1 7
 + 2 · 8 ☐
 ---------
   8 · ☐ 1
```

11.
```
   6 · 4 ☐
 + 2 · ☐ 6
 ---------
   ☐ · 2 3
```

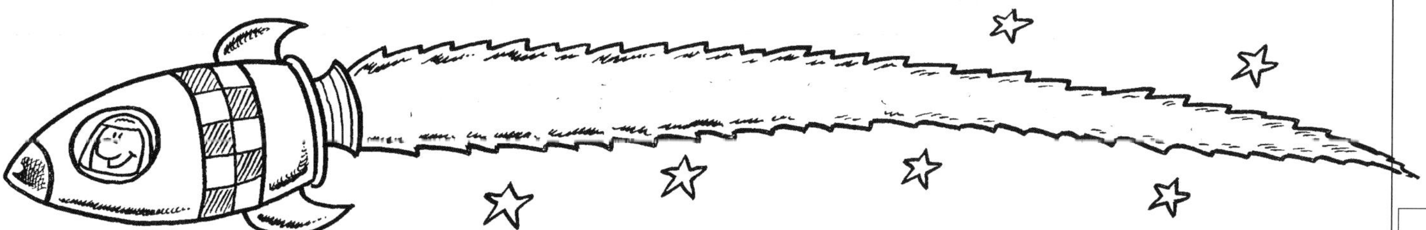

☐ /9

Score: ☐ /22 Total: ☐

Subtraction

Skills summary

- To recognise the relationship between addition and subtraction
- To subtract 2-place decimals using a standard written method

Diagnostic materials

Number Textbook 2, page 60, questions 5 to 11
- Check pupils can write all the addition and subtraction facts using a set of given numbers.

Number Textbook 2, page 65, questions 1 to 7
- Check pupils are able to set out subtractions involving decimal numbers correctly, and subtract 2-place decimals using a standard written method.

Oral questions

1. If 234 + 565 = 799, what is 799 subtract 565?
2. Write an addition sentence to show that 234 – 189 = 45.
3. Find the difference between 12·3 and 7·8.
4. Take 2·45 away from 3·65.

Common difficulties

Pupils may become confused when a calculation is not written down, especially when the two numbers have a different number of digits. Show how aligning the decimal points prevents the numbers from being placed in the wrong columns.

Make the link between addition and subtraction explicit. Use visual images to help pupils make the connection. If using Base Ten apparatus, model the following: *300 add 500 makes 800, so we put the blocks together; if I take 500 away I am left with 300, so we take the blocks away.*

Practice activities

1 Take a handful of coins out of a bag. (Use real or plastic coins – ensure there is a high proportion of high value coins.) Write down the total. Take another handful of coins out of the bag. Find the difference between the first amount and the second amount.

2 Use place-value cards to form two 3-digit numbers. Add them together and write down the number sentence. Write down three more number sentences using the same three numbers.

Answers

1. 234	**2.** 45 + 189 = 234	**3.** 4·5	**4.** 1·2
5. 800	**6.** 186	**7.** 262	**8** and **9** should be ticked
12. 77p	**13.** £1·71 or 171p		

Name ______________________________ **N40** **N41**

1. [ ] **2.** [ ] **3.** [ ] **4.** [ ]

/4

Complete the number sentences.

5. 327 + 473 = ____   ____ − 473 = 327

6. 261 + ____ = 447   447 − ____ = 261

7. ____ + 514 = 776   776 − 514 = ____

/3

Tick the calculations that are correct.

8.
$$\begin{array}{r} 2{\cdot}63 \\ -\ 1{\cdot}76 \\ \hline 0{\cdot}87 \end{array}$$
[ ]

9.
$$\begin{array}{r} 3{\cdot}12 \\ -\ 1{\cdot}46 \\ \hline 1{\cdot}66 \end{array}$$
[ ]

10.
$$\begin{array}{r} 5{\cdot}26 \\ -\ 1{\cdot}57 \\ \hline 4{\cdot}31 \end{array}$$
[ ]

11.
$$\begin{array}{r} 7{\cdot}83 \\ -\ 3{\cdot}68 \\ \hline 4{\cdot}25 \end{array}$$
[ ]

/4

How much will be left in each purse?

12.

____

13.

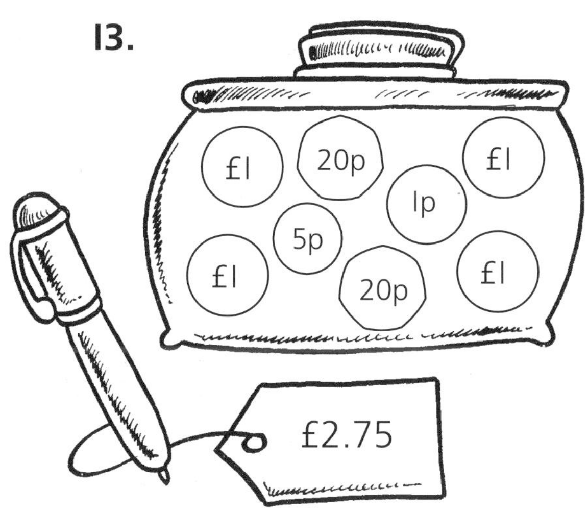

____

/2

Score: [ ] /13   Total: [ ]

Odd, even and square numbers

Skills summary

- To use knowledge of the sum of odd and even numbers
- To use knowledge of the difference between odd and even numbers
- To recognise square numbers
- To calculate square numbers

Diagnostic materials

Number Textbook 2, page 67, questions 1 to 14

- Check pupils are able to recognise whether the answer will be odd or even when more than two numbers are added together.

Number Textbook 2, page 70, questions 1 to 9

- Check pupils can use tables facts to calculate the squares of larger numbers.

Oral questions

1. If I add 33, 35 and 37 will the total be odd or even?
2. 238 – 174 gives an odd answer. True or false?
3. What is 8 squared?
4. I am thinking of a number. I multiply it by itself to get 36. What number did I start with?

Common difficulties

Some pupils struggle to recognise larger odd and even numbers, especially if most of the digits are odd but it is an even number or vice versa, e.g. 152. Pupils need to be reminded that when deciding whether a number is odd or even it is the *last* digit that is most important. Show how a number can be partitioned, e.g. 152 gives 150 + 2; 150 and 2 can each be split exactly in two, so 152 must be able to be split (i.e. is even). Use cubes or squared paper to demonstrate. Provide plenty of practice so that square numbers become instantly recognisable. For example, highlight the square numbers on a multiplication grid and look at the pattern; or write the sequence in the wrong order on the board (include some wrong numbers) and ask pupils to put the numbers in order and decide which are not square numbers.

Practice activities

1 Pick three 2-digit number cards from a pack. If the total would be odd score a point and write down the numbers. Repeat until five points have been scored.

2 Roll a dice ten times. Each time square the number rolled and write down the answer. When ten square numbers have been written down roll the dice again, this time crossing out the square of any number rolled. Continue until all the numbers have been crossed out. How many rolls does it take?

Answers

1. odd **2.** false **3.** 64 **4.** 6
5. any even number **6.** any even number **7.** any odd number
8. any odd number **9.** any even number **10.** any odd number
11. join 5 to 25, 7 to 49, 10 to 100, 6 to 36, 4 to 16
12. 1, 36, 81, 4, 64, 9 should be circled

Name ______________________________

1. [ ] **2.** [ ] **3.** [ ] **4.** [ ]

/4

Complete each calculation to give an even numbered answer.

5. 126 + 120 + ____ **6.** 137 + 123 + ____

7. ____ + 543 + 324 **8.** 123 – ____

9. ____ – 342 **10.** ____ – 341

/6

11. Join each number to its square.

5	49
7	36
10	25
6	100
4	16

/5

12. Circle the square numbers.

1 5 27 36 45 81 4 8 64 9 11 29

/6

Score: ____ /21 Total: ____

Standard units

Skills summary

- To use, read and write standard units of length
- To convert larger to smaller units, and vice versa
- To measure and draw lines to the nearest millimetre

Diagnostic materials

Shape, Data and Measures Textbook, page 3, questions 1 to 16
- Check pupils are able to convert one metric unit to another.

Shape, Data and Measures Textbook, page 4, questions 1 to 10
- Check pupils are able to convert kilometres, centimetres and millimetres to metres.

Oral questions

1. Write 275 cm in metres.
2. Convert $3\frac{1}{2}$ cm into millimetres.
3. How many millimetres are there in one metre?
4. John runs 4750 m in a 5 km race. How many metres has he left to run?

Common difficulties

Pupils need to be clear about the relationship between different metric units. Encourage pupils to work from known facts, e.g. *I know there are 100 cm in 1 m so there must be 200 cm in 2 m and 300 cm in 3 m etc.*

Difficulties may arise when pupils need to convert from a metric unit to a much larger or smaller unit, e.g. converting from metres to millimetres, or centimetres to kilometres. Pupils may find it easier to do the conversion in stages, i.e. convert metres to centimetres then convert the centimetres to millimetres, rather than trying to do the conversion in one jump.

Practice activities

1. Take body measurements, e.g. length of arm, length of leg, circumference of head, arm span, height etc. Write each one in millimetres, centimetres and metres.
2. Roll a ten-sided dice twice to form a 1-place decimal number, e.g. 6·3. Draw a line the corresponding number of centimetres long. Write the length of the line in centimetres and millimetres.

Answers

1. $2\frac{3}{4}$ or 2·75 m **2.** 35 mm **3.** 1000 mm **4.** 250 m

5. top row: 3600 mm, 6900 mm; middle row: 470 cm, 690 cm; bottom row: 3·6 m, 4·7 m

6. top row: 25 000 cm, 250 000 cm; middle row: 500 m, 2500 m; bottom row: $\frac{1}{2}$ km or 0·5 km, $\frac{1}{4}$ km or 0·25 km

7. 2·5 m or 250 cm **8.** 550 cm or 5·5 m **9.** 280 cm or 2·8 m

10. 3·5 m or 350 cm **11.** 2000 mm, 200 cm or 2 m **12.** 450 cm

Name ______________________________

1. [ ] 2. [ ] 3. [ ] 4. [ ]

/4

5. Complete the table below to show equivalent lengths.

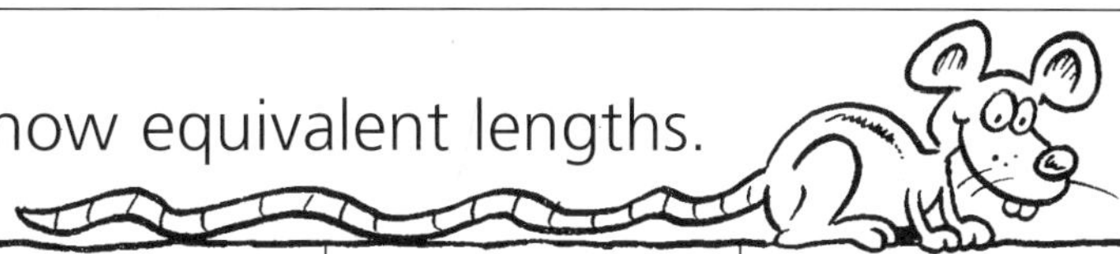

Millimetres	2000 mm		4700 mm	
Centimetres	200 cm	360 cm		
Metres	2 m			6·9 m

/6

6. Complete the table below to show equivalent lengths.

Centimetres	100 000 cm	50 000 cm		
Metres	1000 m		250 m	
Kilometres	1 km			2·5 km

/6

Complete these calculations.

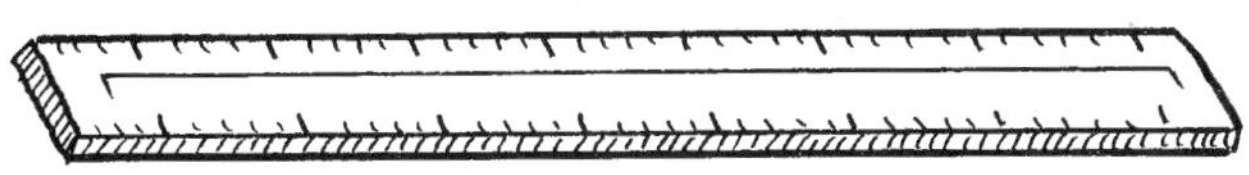

7. 2·5 m + _____ = 5 m

8. 150 cm + _____ = 7 m

9. 320 cm + _____ = 6 m

10. 4·5 m + _____ = 800 cm

11. 3000 mm + _____ = 5 m

12. 1500 mm + 3 m = _____ cm

/6

Score: [ ] /22 Total: [ ]

Standard units

Skills summary

- To use, read and write standard units of weight
- To convert larger to smaller units, and vice versa
- To suggest suitable units to measure different weights
- To read measures from scales

Diagnostic materials

Shape, Data and Measures Textbook, page 6
- Check pupils are able to convert kilograms to grams, and vice versa.

Shape, Data and Measures Textbook, page 8, questions 1 to 6
- Check pupils are able to choose an appropriate weight for each item.

Oral questions

1. How many grams are there in 1·6 kg?
2. Write 3500 grams in kilograms.
3. George takes a 2 kg bag of sugar from the shelf. He uses $\frac{1}{2}$ kg in a recipe. How much sugar is left in the bag? Write your answer in grams.
4. Which is an appropriate weight for an apple: 10 g, 100 g or 1000 g?

Common difficulties

Pupils need opportunities to carry out plenty of practical work when developing an understanding of weight. It is important when working on estimation skills that pupils are given the opportunity to compare weights against given benchmarks.

Use number lines marked with different scales to help develop pupils' understanding of scale, and encourage them to think about the value of intermittent points.

Practice activities

1 Look at a recipe from a recipe book. Write each measurement in kilograms (if written in grams) and in grams (if written in kilograms).

2 Estimate the weight of five objects. Mark each estimate on a scale drawn on a piece of paper (similar to those on the Photocopy Master). After each estimate weigh the object and mark the real weight on the scale. Calculate the difference between the estimate and the actual weight.

Answers

1. 1600 g **2.** 3·5 kg **3.** 1500 g **4.** 100 g
5. 800 g or 0·8 kg **6.** 550 g or 0·55 kg **7.** 1400 g or 1·4 kg **8.** 900 g or 0·9 kg
9. join 750 g to $\frac{3}{4}$ kg, 36 kg to 36 000 g, 2·5 kg to 2500 g, 3600 g to 3·6 kg, circle 360 g and 7·5 kg

Name ______________________ **M2**

1. [ ] **2.** [ ] **3.** [ ] **4.** [ ]

/4

Write the amount shown on each scale.

5.

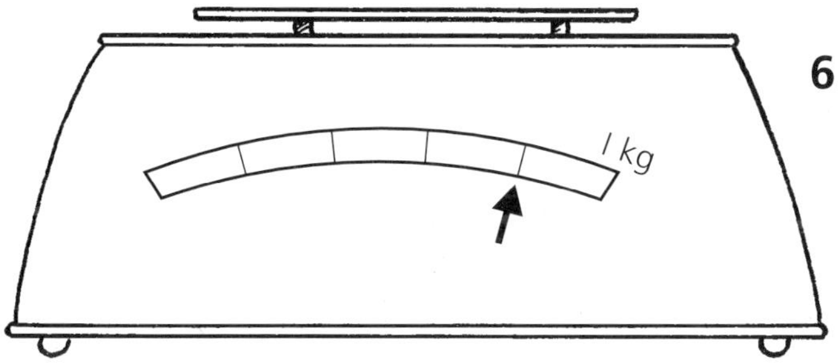

6.

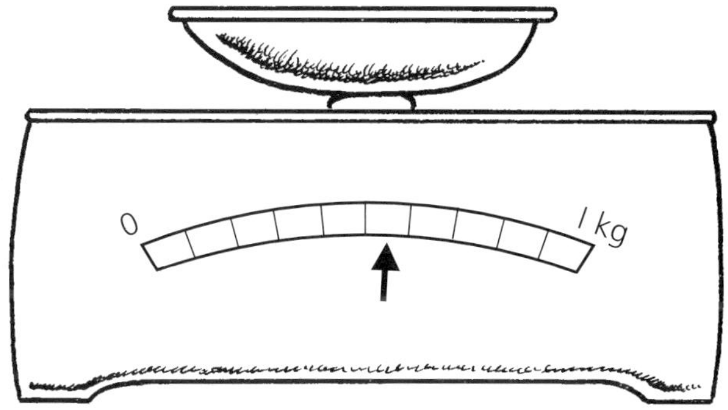

7.

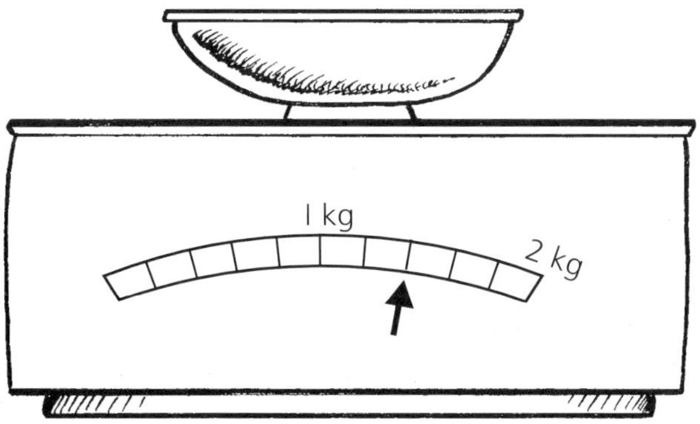

8.

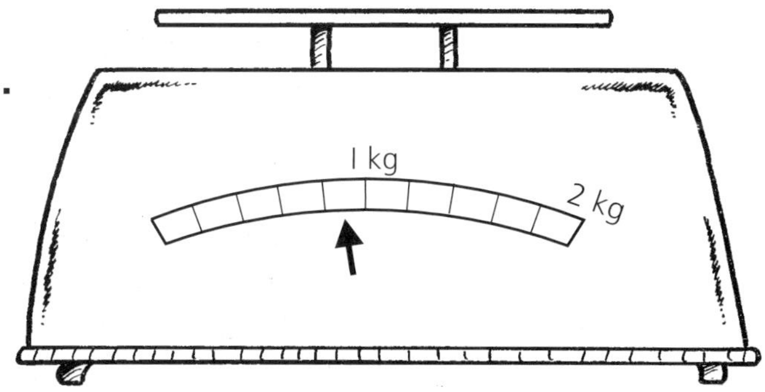

/4

---

9. Join weights that are equal. Circle the weights that cannot be joined.

750 g	7·5 kg	$\frac{3}{4}$ kg	36 000 g	3600 g
360 g	2·5 kg	36 kg	3·6 kg	2500 g

/6

Score: [ ] /14 Total: [ ]

Area and perimeter

Skills summary

- To understand area measured in square centimetres
- To understand and use the formula in words 'length times breadth' for the area of a rectangle
- To understand, measure and calculate the perimeter of a rectangle
- To understand, measure and calculate the perimeter of a regular polygon

Diagnostic materials

Shape, Data and Measures Textbook, page 10, questions 1 to 10

- Check pupils are able to find given areas by using the formula 'length times breadth'.

Shape, Data and Measures Textbook, page 14, questions 1 to 10

- Check pupils are able to find the length of a missing side in a rectangle by using the perimeter and the length of a known side.

Oral questions

1. Find the area of a rectangle with a length of 6 cm and breadth of 5 cm.
2. A rectangle has an area of 24 cm^2. If it has a length of 8 cm, what is its breadth?
3. A square has a perimeter of 20 cm. Find the length of one of its sides.
4. The length of each side on a regular hexagon is 7 cm. Calculate its perimeter.

Common difficulties

When pupils first begin calculating area by multiplying the length by the breadth make the connection with counting squares explicit, i.e. draw a rectangle 3 rows by 4 columns; point out that there are 3 rows, each with 4 squares, so to find the number of squares it is quicker to calculate 3 × 4 than to count the squares, especially when dealing with larger numbers.

Encourage pupils to use what they know when finding the perimeter of regular shapes, e.g. when finding the perimeter of a regular pentagon measure the length of one side (so you know the length of each side), then multiply it by 5.

Practice activities

1 Choose a 2-digit number card from a set showing multiples of 12 up to 48. Roll a six-sided dice. If five or one is rolled roll again. The 2-digit number represents the area, the dice roll represents the breadth. Calculate the length, then draw the rectangle.

2 Find the perimeter of regular shapes by drawing round templates and measuring the sides. Use a calculator to find the total length if necessary.

Answers

1. 30 cm^2	**2.** 3 cm	**3.** 5 cm	**4.** 42 cm
5. 5 m	**6.** 3 cm	**7.** 7 cm	**8.** 8 m

9. top row: 15 cm^2, 16 cm middle row: 28 cm^2, 22 cm
bottom row: 16 cm^2, 20 cm

Name ______________________________

M3 **M4**

1. ☐ **2.** ☐ **3.** ☐ **4.** ☐

☐ /4

Calculate the length of each side of these regular shapes from the perimeter.

5.

Perimeter = 20 m
Each side = _____ m

6.

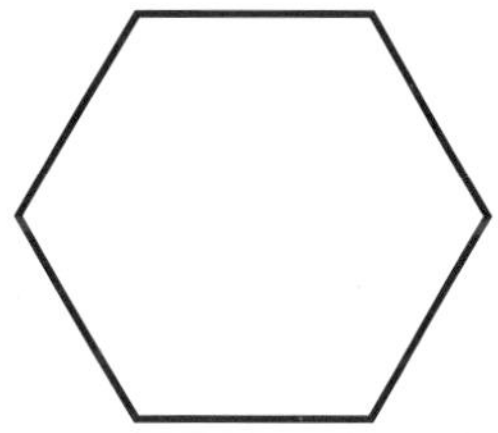

Perimeter = 18 cm
Each side = _____ cm

7.

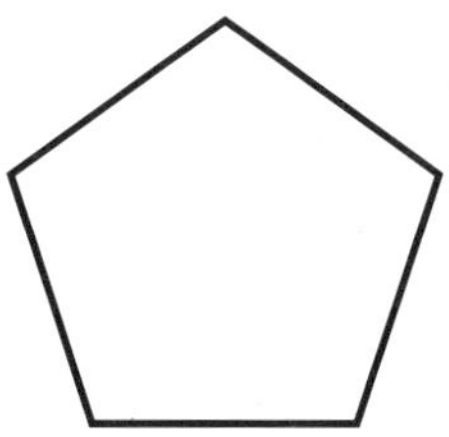

Perimeter = 35 cm
Each side = _____ cm

8.

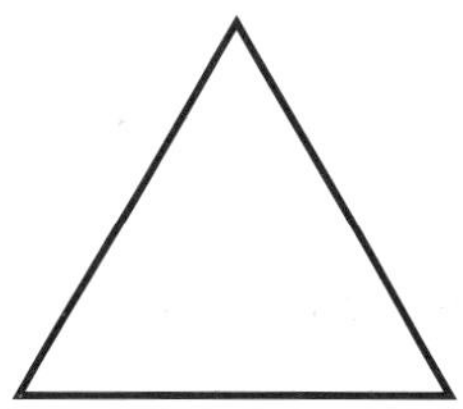

Perimeter = 24 m
Each side = _____ m

☐ /4

Complete the table to calculate the area and perimeter of each rectangle.

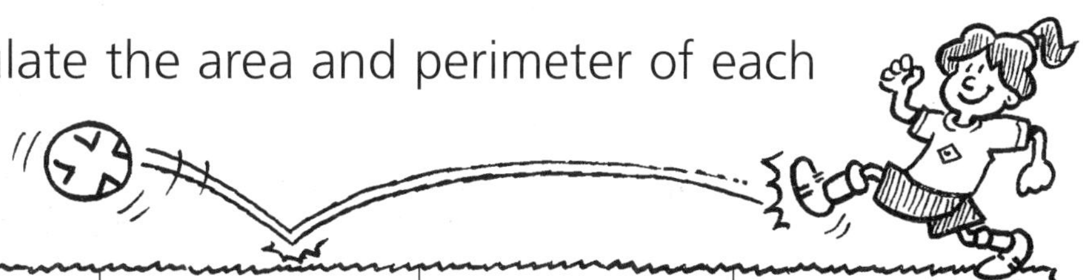

	Length	Breadth	Area	Perimeter
Rectangle 1	5 cm	3 cm		
Rectangle 2	7 cm	4 cm		
Rectangle 3	8 cm	2 cm		

☐ /6

Score: ☐ /14 Total: ☐

Standard units

Skills summary

- To use, read and write standard units of capacity
- To convert larger to smaller units, and vice versa
- To suggest suitable units to measure different capacities
- To read measures from scales

Diagnostic materials

Shape, Data and Measures Textbook, page 15
- Check pupils can convert millilitres to litres, and vice versa.

Shape, Data and Measures Textbook, page 16, questions 1 to 9
- Check pupils are able to select the appropriate capacity for a range of containers.

Oral questions

1. A bottle contains 0·75 l. How many millilitres is that?
2. How many 250 ml containers would it take to fill a $1\frac{1}{2}$ l bottle?
3. (Hold up a jar with a capacity of about 500 ml). Will this jar hold 50 ml, 500 ml, or 5 l of liquid?
4. A jug holds 3 l of water. 1500 ml is poured out. How much is left in the jug?

Common difficulties

Pupils need plenty of opportunity to estimate and measure capacities of different containers. It is important that they use a range of different measuring jugs with different scales so that they are able to choose an appropriate jug to measure the capacity of a given container. For example, discuss with pupils why it is inappropriate to use a 1 l measuring jug to measure approximately 50 ml of water.

Encourage the pupils to make connections with units of measurement that they know, e.g. converting grams to kilograms, metres to kilometres and millilitres to litres all require pupils to divide by 1000.

Practice activities

1 Collect six different containers that have a capacity of between $\frac{1}{2}$ l and 1 l. Put the containers in order of size and estimate the capacity of each. Now measure the capacity of each container. How many changes need to be made to the order of the containers?

2 Find five containers and estimate their capacity. Then match each to an appropriate measuring jug. Finally measure the capacity of each. How close were your estimates?

Answers

1. 750 ml **2.** 6 **3.** 500 ml **4.** 1·5 l, $1\frac{1}{2}$ l or 1500 ml
5. 500 ml = 0·5 l **6.** 800 ml = 0·8 l **7.** 1200 ml = 1·2 l
8. 2400 ml = 2·4 l
9. 5 **10.** 4 **11.** 12

Name ________________________________ **M5**

1. [ ] **2.** [ ] **3.** [ ] **4.** [ ]

[ ] / 4

Write the amount shown in each jug in millilitres (ml) and litres (l).

5.

_____ ml = _____ l

6.

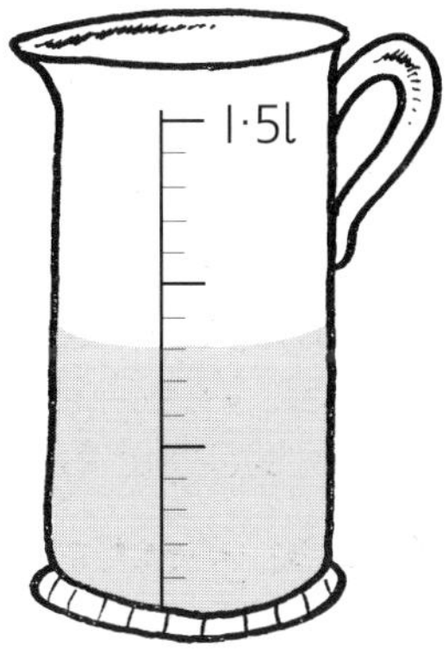

_____ ml = _____ l

7.

_____ ml = _____ l

8.

_____ ml = _____ l

[ ] / 8

Calculate how many smaller bottles it would take to fill the larger one.

9.

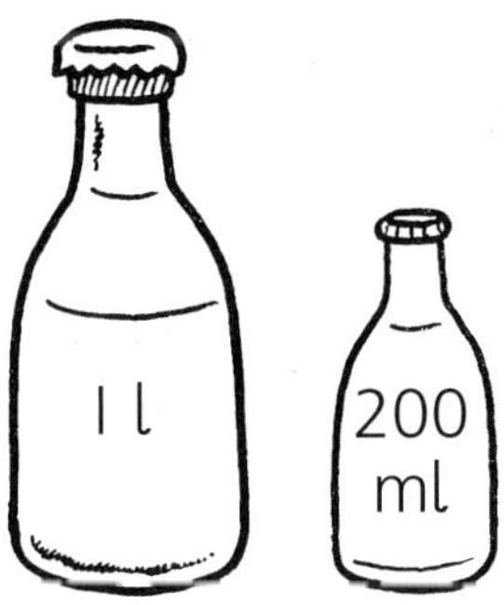

____

10.

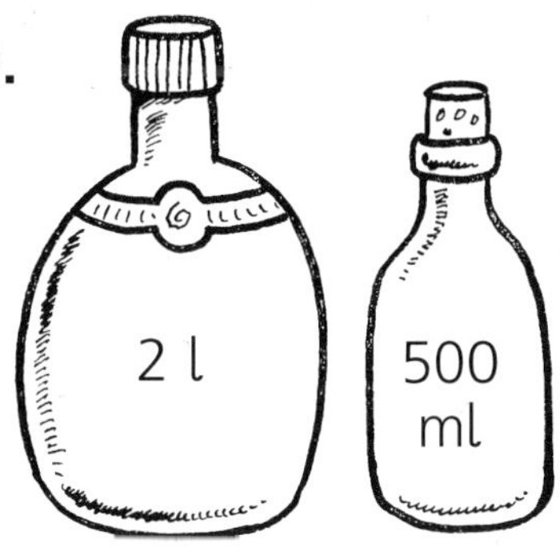

____

11.

____

[ ] / 3

Score: [ ] / 15 Total: [ ]

Time

Skills summary

- To use, read and write units of time
- To convert units from larger to smaller units, and vice versa
- To use, read and write times using the 24-hour clock
- To use a timetable

Diagnostic materials

Shape, Data and Measures Textbook, page 19, questions 1 to 10
- Check pupils can convert units of time to hours.

Shape, Data and Measures Textbook, page 21, questions 1 to 13
- Check pupils are able to convert times from the 12-hour clock to the 24-hour clock.

Oral questions

1. How many hours in two days?
2. Convert five hours to minutes.
3. The time is 14:50. What time is that on a 12-hour clock?
4. If it is 4:15 p.m. what time will a 24-hour clock show?

Common difficulties

Pupils can find it difficult to convert one unit of time to another as it requires multiplying or dividing by more complex numbers (60, 24 etc.) than conversions of other units of measurement. Provide pupils with plenty of opportunity to practise useful number skills, e.g. counting in steps of 60, looking at numbers divisible by 24 etc. Encourage pupils to use facts that they already know, e.g. how many hours in three days? There are 24 hours in one, 48 hours in two, and so 72 in three.

Practice activities

1 Look at a train timetable that shows 24-hour clock times. For three journeys write: the time and place of departure; time and place of arrival; journey time. Then write each of the times as they would appear on a 12-hour clock.

2 Choose a number card from a set showing numbers 0–23, and one from a selection showing multiples of 5 (up to 60). The first card represents the number of hours, the second represents the number of minutes. Write down the time, and then write it in as many different ways as possible, e.g. 15:45, 3:45 p.m., quarter to 4, 45 minutes past 3 etc.

Answers

1. 48 hours **2.** 300 minutes **3.** 2:50 p.m. **4.** 16:15

5. join a to i, b to g, c to f, d to h, e to j

6a. Sport **6b.** Soap Opera **6c.** Quiz Show **6d.** Film

7a. 4:30 p.m. **7b.** 7:30 p.m. **7c.** 4:05 p.m. **7d.** 5:05 p.m.

Name ______________________ **M6** **M7**

1. ☐ **2.** ☐ **3.** ☐ **4.** ☐

☐ /4

5. Join equivalent amounts of time.

a	$3\frac{1}{2}$ hours	**f**	6000 seconds
b	$2\frac{1}{2}$ days	**g**	60 hours
c	100 minutes	**h**	7200 seconds
d	2 hours	**i**	210 minutes
e	2 days	**j**	2880 minutes

☐ /5

6. Use the TV Guide to work out what is on at:

a 12:15 p.m. ______________

b 7 p.m. ______________

c 6:05 p.m. ______________

d 10:30 a.m. ______________

TV Guide

10:30	Film
12:15	Sport
16:05	News
16:30	Cartoons
17:05	Documentary
18:05	Quiz Show
19:00	Soap Opera
19:30	Cookery Show

7. When are these programmes on? Write your answers as 12-hour clock times.

a Cartoons ______________ **b** Cookery Show ______________

c News ______________ **d** Documentary ______________

☐ /8

Score: ☐ /17 Total: ☐

2-d shape and symmetry

Skills summary

- To use the terms 'vertical' and 'horizontal'
- To recognise parallel and perpendicular lines
- To recognise lines of symmetry in regular polygons
- To draw the reflection of shapes in a mirror line

Diagnostic materials

Shape, Data and Measures Textbook, page 25, questions 1 to 12
- Check pupils are able to recognise horizontal and vertical lines.

Shape, Data and Measures Textbook, page 27, questions 5 to 10
- Check pupils can recognise lines that are parallel or perpendicular to a given side.

Shape, Data and Measures Textbook, page 35, questions 10 to 16
- Check pupils are able to complete patterns to give two lines of symmetry.

Oral questions

1. On the letter I, indicate with an arrow the vertical line or lines.
2. Draw a line parallel to the one shown.
3. Draw a four-sided shape which has a least two sides perpendicular to one another.
4. If a double-sided mirror is put onto the mirror line which two letters will be revealed?

Common difficulties

Pupils may find it difficult to reflect shapes in a mirror line. Remind them that the image of the shape must be an equal distance from the mirror line. They may find it useful to use a mirror to support or check their reflection – but remind them to draw on the paper what they see in the mirror and not to assume that because they see an accurate reflection in the mirror it is accurate on the paper.

When completing symmetrical patterns remind pupils that the mirror line reflects both ways. This means that coloured squares on both sides must have the equivalent square on the opposite side coloured, irrespective of whether the original coloured square is on the left or the right.

Practice activities

1 Draw round shape templates to generate some 2-d shapes. Write a description of each using properties such as 'parallel sides' and 'number of lines of symmetry'.

2 Divide an 8 × 8 square into quarters using two mirror lines. Draw a pattern in one quadrant and reflect it in each of the mirror lines.

Answers

1. check vertical line indicated
2. check a parallel line has been drawn
3. check pupils have drawn an appropriate shape **4.** M, X
6, 7 and **8** should be ticked **11.** join a to e, b to g, c to h, d to f

Name ______________________________ **S1** **S4**

1.  **2.** 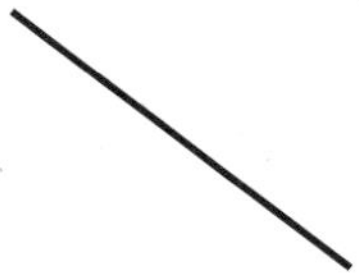 **3.** **4.** 

/4

Tick the shapes which have at least one pair of parallel sides.

5. 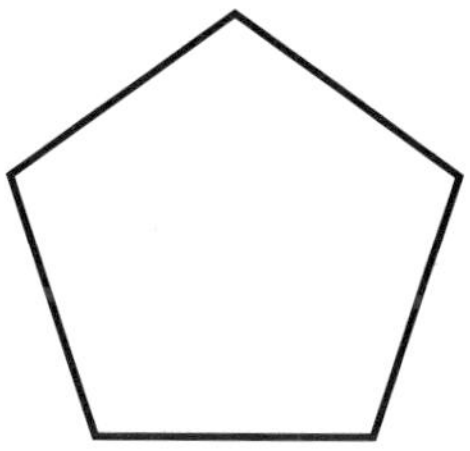 ☐ **6.** 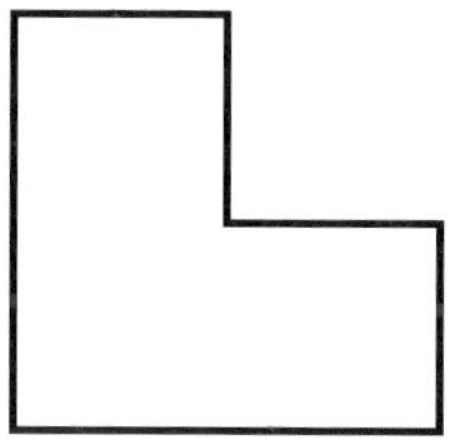 ☐ **7.**  ☐

8. 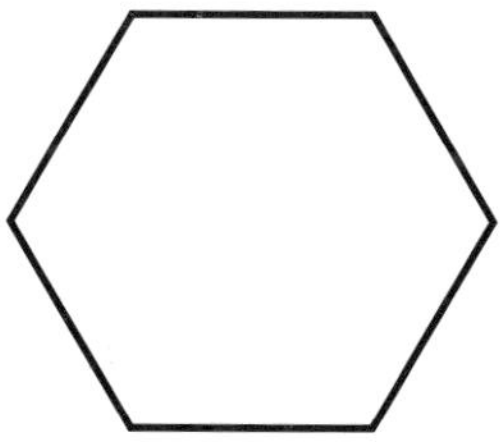 ☐ **9.** 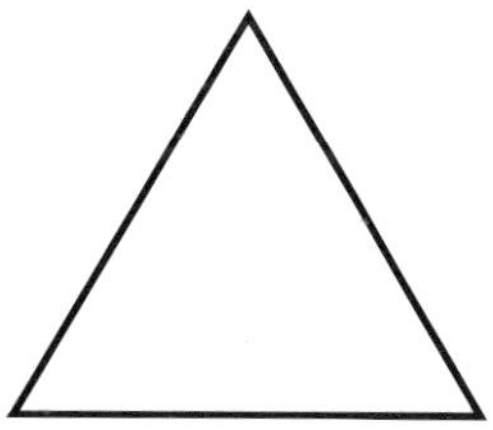 ☐ **10.** 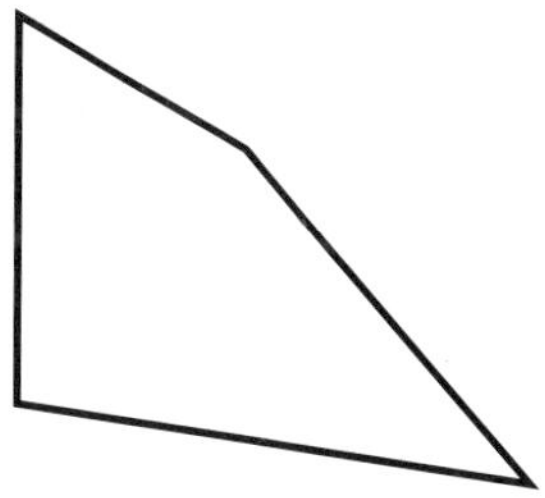 ☐

/6

11. Join the descriptions to the correct shapes.

a two pairs of parallel sides, four right angles, two lines of symmetry

b two pairs of parallel sides, four right angles, four lines of symmetry

c two pairs of parallel sides, no right angles, no lines of symmetry

d one pair of parallel sides, no right angles, one line of symmetry

e 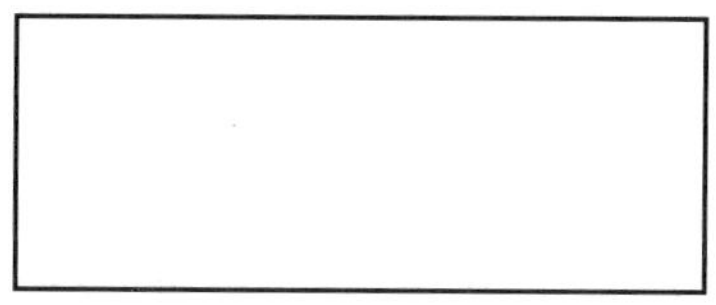

f 

g 

h 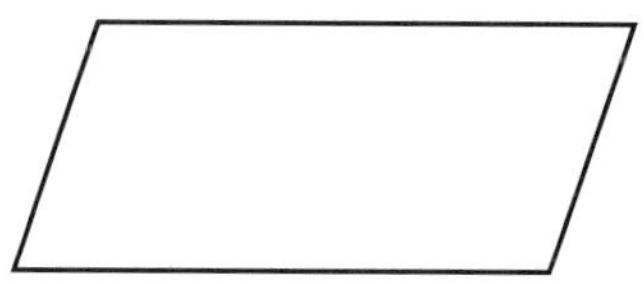

/4

Score: ____ /14 Total: ____

2-d shape

Skills summary

- To name 2-d shapes
- To recognise properties of 2-d shapes
- To recognise diagonals in 2-d shapes
- To name and classify triangles
- To recognise properties of different triangles

Diagnostic materials

Shape, Data and Measures Textbook, page 29, questions 1 to 16

- Check pupils are able to name polygons and recognise whether they are regular or irregular.

Shape, Data and Measures Textbook, page 33, questions 1 to 13

- Check pupils can name and classify different types of triangle.

Oral questions

1. Name the shape.
2. Draw the diagonals on the shape.
3. Draw a right-angled, scalene triangle.
4. What sort of triangle has two sides the same length, and two equal angles?

Common difficulties

Pupils can become confused with words that have different but similar meaning in common usage, e.g. diagonal. It is important that they have opportunities to draw diagonals and refer to diagonals when working with 2-d polygons. Difficulties may arise if pupils have only experienced polygons in one orientation – they need to see polygons in different orientations to understand that the shape is the same, regardless of whether it appears to be on its base or not.

Practical activities

1 Throw a ten-sided dice. Draw a shape with that number of sides. Repeat several times.

2 Draw a Carroll diagram, with 'right-angled' and 'not right-angled' as headings, 'scalene', 'equilateral' and 'isosceles' down the side. Draw a triangle in each box. In which box is it impossible to draw a triangle?

Answers

1. irregular hexagon
2. check all five diagonals have been drawn correctly on the shape
3. check the triangle has been drawn accurately
4. isosceles
5. top left cell: c, e; top right cell: d, f; bottom left cell: a, h; bottom right cell: b, g
6, 7, and **9** should be ticked

Name ______________________ **S2** **S3**

1. 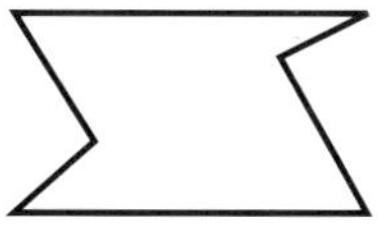 ____________ **2.** 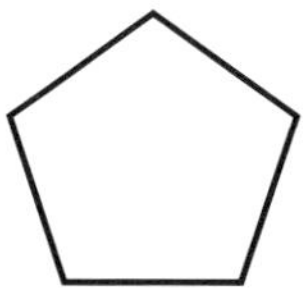 **3.** **4.** 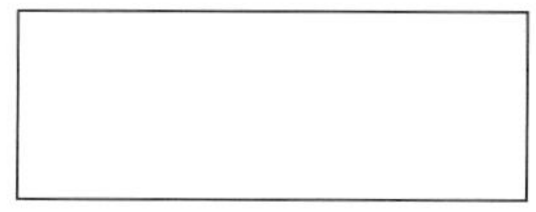

4

5. Write the correct letter for each shape in the Carroll diagram.

a 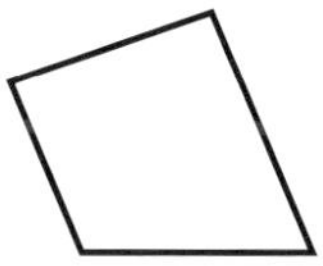 **b** 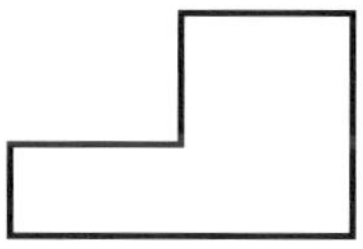 **c**  **d** 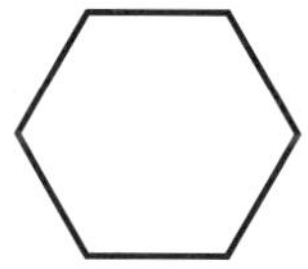

e 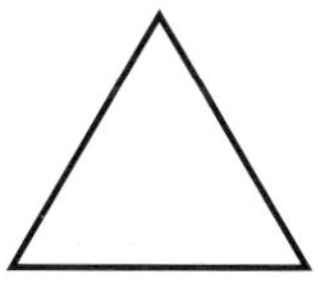 **f** 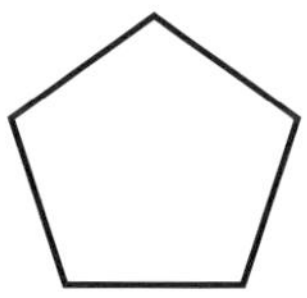 **g** 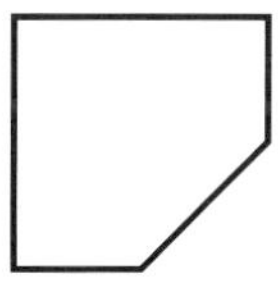 **h** 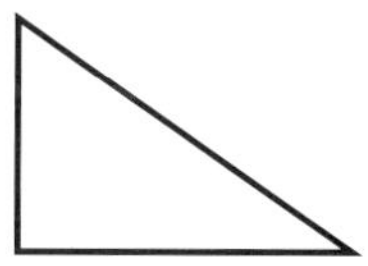

	Fewer than five sides	Five sides or more
Regular		
Irregular		

8

Tick the isosceles triangles.

6. 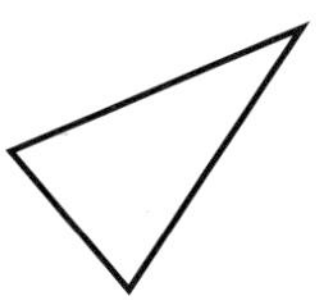 **7.** 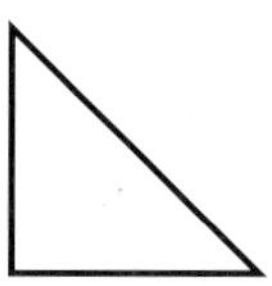 **8.** 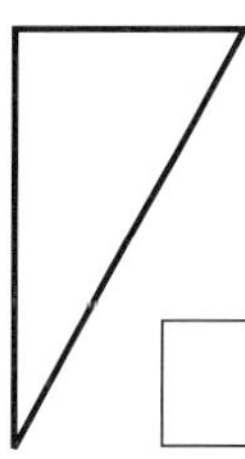 **9.** 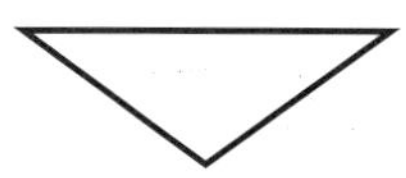

4

Score: /16 Total:

3-d shape

Skills summary

- To name common 3-d shapes
- To recognise properties of 3-d shapes
- To classify 3-d shapes according to their properties

Diagnostic materials

Shape, Data and Measures Textbook, page 37, questions 12 to 19
- Check pupils are able to name prisms and pyramids according to the shapes of the base or end faces.

Shape, Data and Measures Textbook, page 38, questions 1 to 9
- Check pupils are able to recognise the shapes that will be constructed from given nets.

Oral questions

1. How many faces does a square-based pyramid have?
2. I am thinking of a shape. It has five faces: three are rectangular, two are triangular, and it has six vertices. What shape am I thinking of?
3. What sort of prism has eight faces?
4. Is a cone a polyhedron?

Common difficulties

Some pupils may have difficulty visualising 3-d shapes from 2-d drawings. Provide solid shapes for pupils to work with if they are describing or investigating properties of 3-d shapes. Ensure pupils have opportunities to look at similarities and differences between shapes and to sort shapes into families. Encourage them to make generalisations by asking questions such as *What makes a prism a prism? Is a cylinder a prism?*

Practice activities

1 Choose five solids and write a description to go with each one. Make sure the description could not match any another shape.

2 Draw a chart with headings such as: name of shape, number of faces, shape of faces, number of vertices, sketch of the net etc. Use the table to classify four different shapes.

Answers

1. 5 **2.** triangular prism **3.** hexagonal prism **4.** no
6. triangular prism, 5 faces **7.** cylinder, 3 faces
8. square-based pyramid, 5 faces **9.** sphere, 1 face **10.** cone, 2 faces
11, 12, 14 and **15** should be ticked

Name ______________________________ **S5**

1. [ ] **2.** [ ]

3. [ ] **4.** [ ]

/4

Name each shape and write the number of faces each one has.

5. 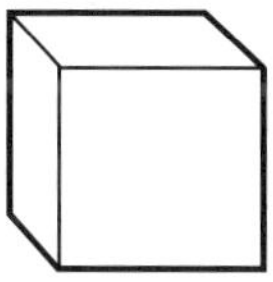

cube

6 faces

6. 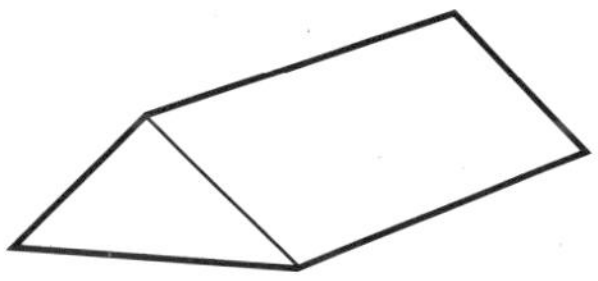

____

______ faces

7. 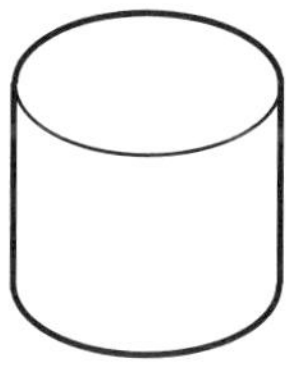

____

______ faces

8. 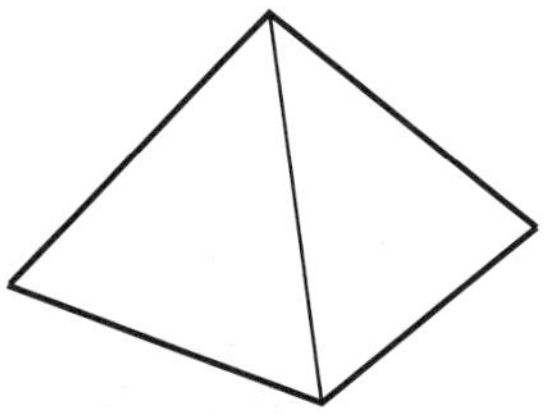

____

______ faces

9. 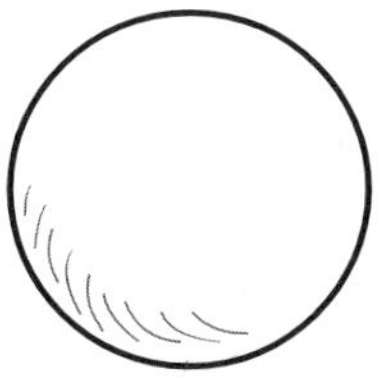

____

______ faces

10. 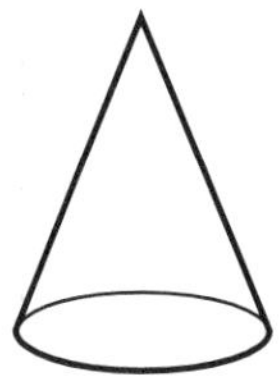

____

______ faces

/5

Tick the shapes that are prisms.

11. 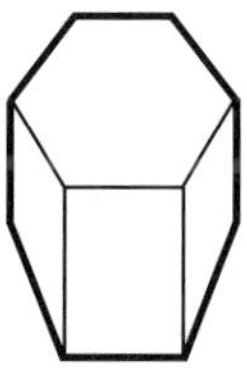 [ ]

12. 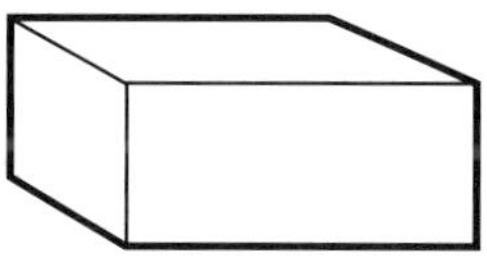 [ ]

13. 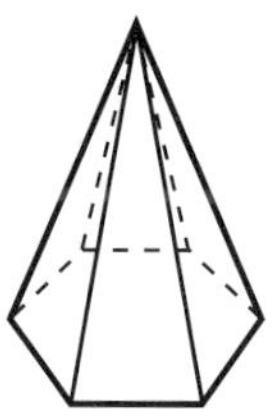 [ ]

14.  [ ]

15. 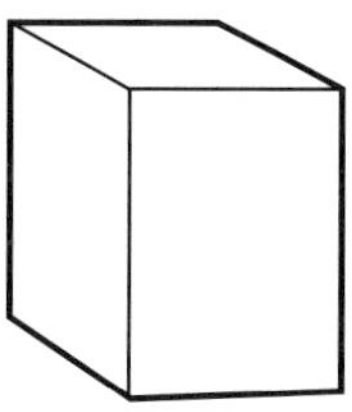 [ ]

16. 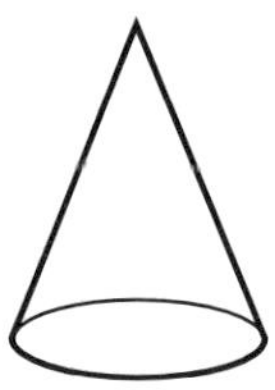 [ ]

/4

Score: [ ] /13 Total: [ ]

Rotation and coordinates

Skills summary

- To recognise the position of shapes after given rotations
- To read and plot coordinates in the first quadrant
- To draw polygons by plotting the coordinates of their vertices

Diagnostic materials

Shape, Data and Measures Textbook, page 42, questions 1 to 9
- Check pupils are able to draw shapes in the correct position after given rotations.

Shape, Data and Measures Textbook, page 44, questions 1 to 15
- Check pupils can plot coordinates in the first quadrant.

Oral questions

1. Draw the shape after a 90° clockwise rotation.
2. (Draw a grid on the board. Mark on the point (3, 7).) Write down the coordinates of this point.
3. Write down the coordinates of a point two to the left of the one marked on the grid.
4. (Write the points (2, 4) (4, 4) (2, 2) on the board.) These three points represent three corners of a square. Write down the coordinates of the missing corner.

Common difficulties

Pupils may find it difficult to visualise the orientation of a shape after rotation. They may find it useful to use tracing paper to trace the shape and then rotate the tracing paper. Model this process using an OHP if you are working with the whole class.

When working with coordinates confusion arises over the correct order of the coordinates. Use phrases such as 'along the corridor and up the stairs' or 'crawl before you climb' to reinforce the correct order.

Practice activities

1 Draw different shapes made up of five squares (pentominoes). Rotate each one through 90°, 180°, 270° and draw them again after each rotation.

2 Draw a 10 × 10 grid. On the grid plot points to form a square, a triangle, a pentagon and a hexagon. Write down the coordinates of each shape.

Answers

1. check the shape has been drawn accurately

2. (3, 7) **3.** (1, 7) **4.** (4, 2)

5. a and c should be shaded **6.** a and b should be shaded

7. c and d should be shaded **8.** A (2, 4), B (2, 10), C (6, 8)

Name ______________________________ **S6** **S7**

1. 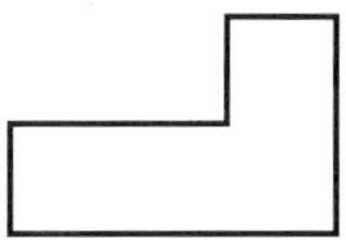

2. (,) **3.** (,) **4.** (,)

/4

Shade the shapes that are rotations of the first shape.

5.

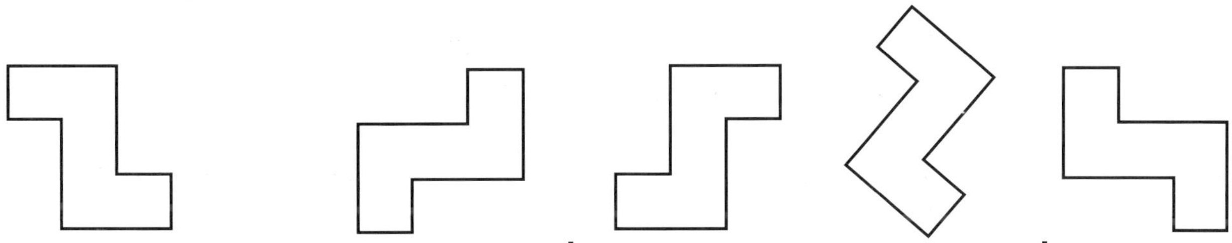

6.

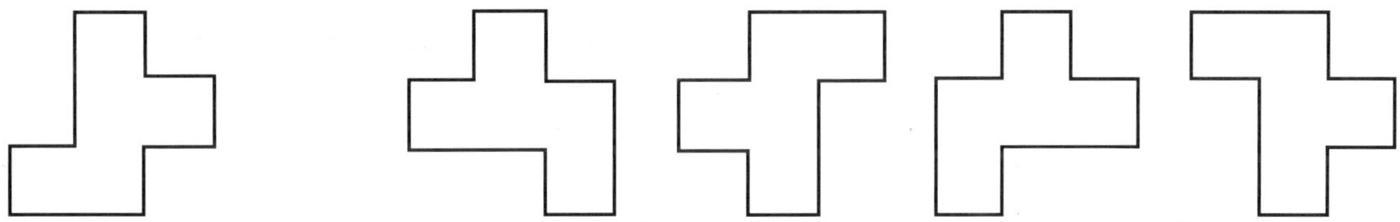

7.

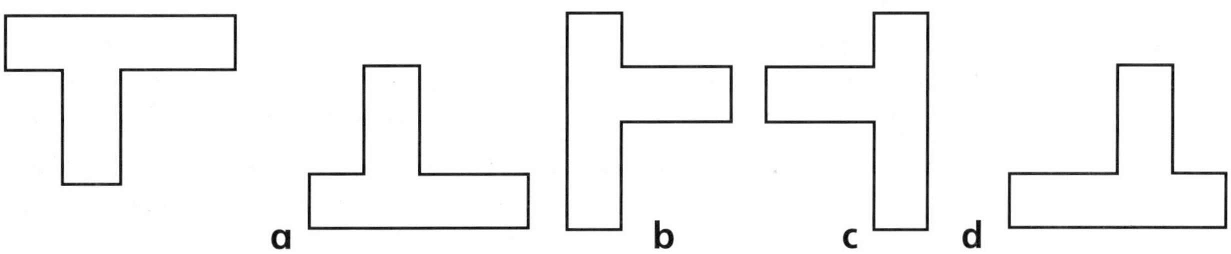

/6

8. Write in the missing coordinates.

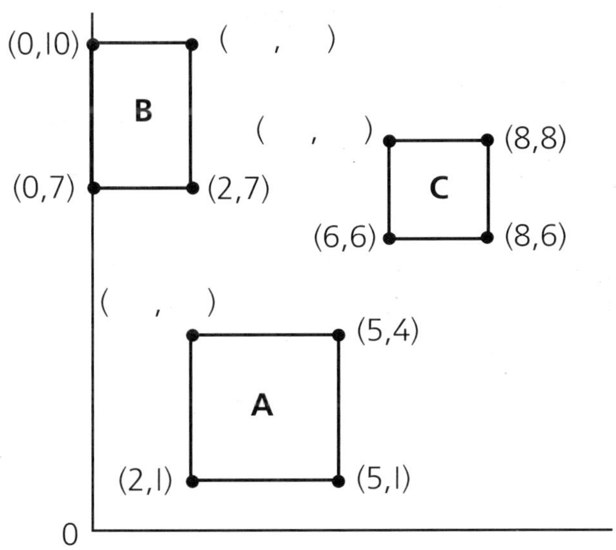

/3

Score: /13 Total:

Angle

Skills summary

- To recognise the relationship between degrees and right angles
- To calculate angles in a straight line
- To measure angles using a protractor
- To draw angles using a protractor
- To estimate an angle in degrees

Diagnostic materials

Shape, Data and Measures Textbook, page 48, questions 1 to 4

- Check pupils are able to decide whether angles are greater than or less than 90° or 180°.

Shape, Data and Measures Textbook, page 49

- Check pupils are able to calculate the size of an unknown angle using knowledge of the number of degrees in a right angle or straight line.

Oral questions

1. Estimate the size of the angle.
2. Which angle is larger than a right angle: 45°, 56°, 89°, 134°?
3. A clock hand has turned 30° to reach five past the hour. How much further does it have to turn to reach quarter past the hour?
4. Which two angles when added would give a straight line: 120°, 70°, 50°, 60°?

Common difficulties

When using a protractor it is common for pupils to line it up inaccurately or to use the wrong scale. Use a protractor on an OHP (or a photocopy of a protractor which avoids blurred edges) to demonstrate how to use a protractor. To ensure pupils use the correct scale, encourage them to estimate first, using their knowledge of the size of right angles and straight lines, e.g. *Is the angle greater than 90°?* Encourage them to refer back to their estimate to check that their answer makes sense.

Practice activities

1 Pick a card from a selection of 2-digit number cards showing multiples of 5 to 100. Draw an angle of the size shown without using a protractor. Then use a protractor to see how close the angle drawn is.

2 Draw six angles of less than 180°. Measure their size, then calculate how much more they would need to turn to make a straight line.

Answers

1. 50° (give a mark for answers in the range 40°–60°) **2.** 134° **3.** 60°
4. 120° and 60°
5. 130° **6.** 55° **7.** 65° **8.** 115° **9.** 160° **10.** 95° **11** and **12** should be ticked
15. check the triangle is drawn accurately: sides 6 cm, 4 cm, 7·2 cm; angles 90°, 35°, 55°

Name ______________________________

S8 S9

I. 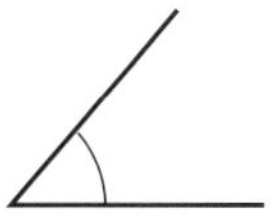

2.

3.

4.

/4

Calculate the missing angles.

5. 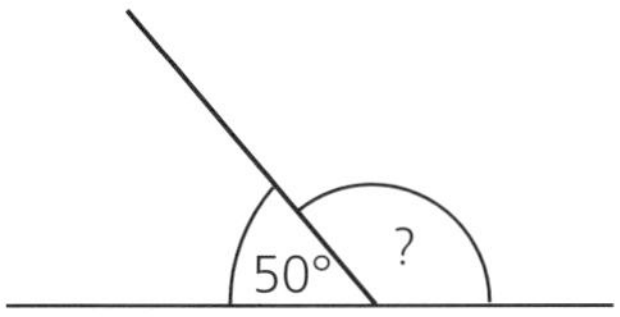

6. 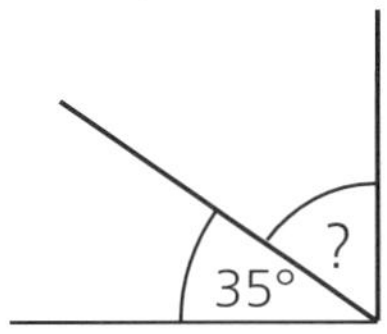

7. 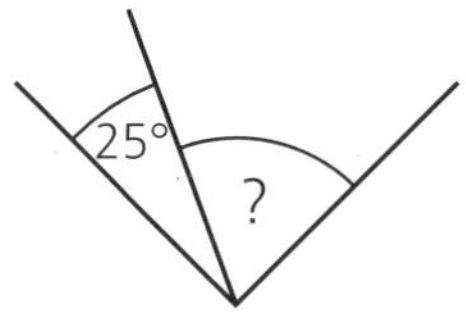

8. 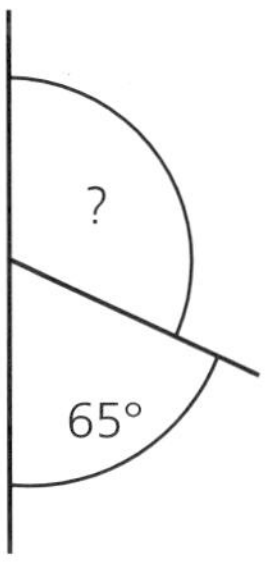

9. 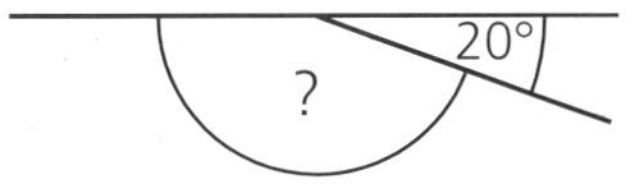

10. 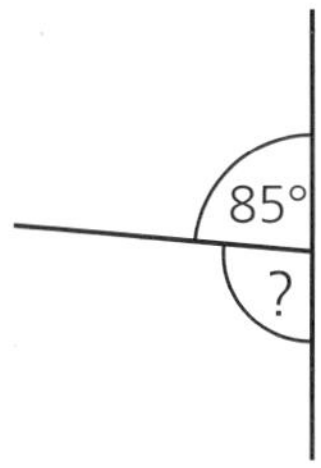

/6

Tick the angles that have been drawn accurately.

II. 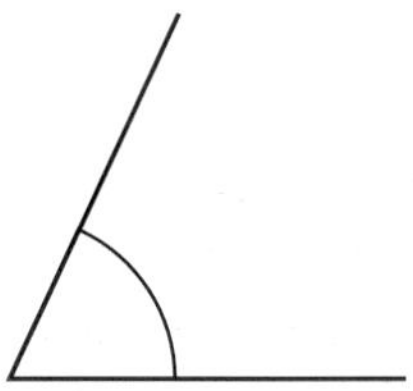

65° ☐

12. 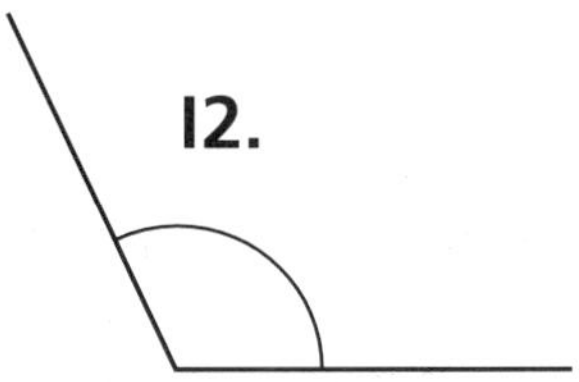

115° ☐

13. 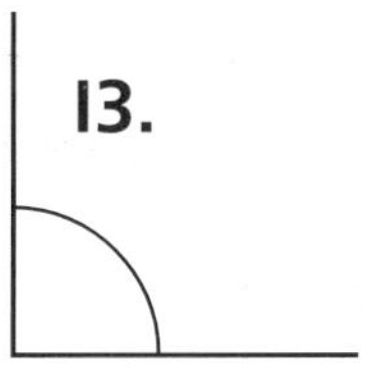

35° ☐

14. 

130° ☐

/4

Draw the triangle again, but with each side twice as long as before.
One side has been done for you.

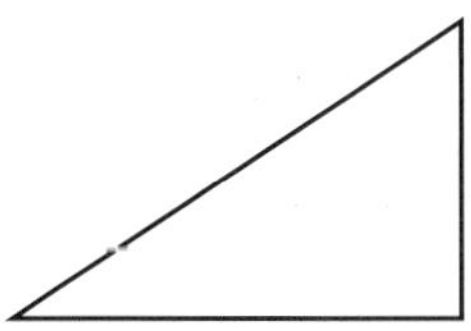

/2

Score: ☐ /16 Total: ☐

Angle

Skills summary

- To recognise acute, obtuse and reflex angles
- To recognise acute and obtuse angles in shapes

Diagnostic materials

Shape, Data and Measures Textbook, page 53, questions 1 to 13
- Check pupils are able to recognise acute, obtuse and reflex angles.

Shape, Data and Measures Textbook, page 54, questions 1 to 13
- Check pupils are able to recognise different types of angles in polygons.

Oral questions

1. Which of these angles is acute: 95°, 73°, 120°?
2. (Draw an obtuse angle on the board.) What sort of angle is this?
3. The minute hand on the clock moves from quarter past to ten to. What type of angle is that turn?
4. What type of angle are the internal angles of an equilateral triangle?

Common difficulties

Remembering the names of the different types of angle can be tricky. Encourage pupils to look for different types of angle around the classroom and to label them using the correct terminology. Draw angles on the board and ask pupils to say everything they can about them, e.g. *it is bigger than a right angle but smaller than a straight line so it is an obtuse angle. It is about 130°.* Refer to the angles formed by the hands on the clock or opening the door.

Practice activities

1 Draw round a number of different 2-d shape templates. Draw up a key for different types of angle, e.g. green = acute, red = obtuse, etc. Colour the internal angles according to the key.

2 Draw four irregular octagons and write a description of each. Make sure each description could only be matched to one of the octagons.

Answers

1. 73° **2.** obtuse **3.** reflex **4.** acute

6, 8, 9, 11 and 12 should be ticked **13.** join a to f, b to h, c to e, d to g

Name ______________________________

S10

1. ☐ **2.** ☐ **3.** ☐ **4.** ☐

/4

Tick the obtuse angles.

5.

6.

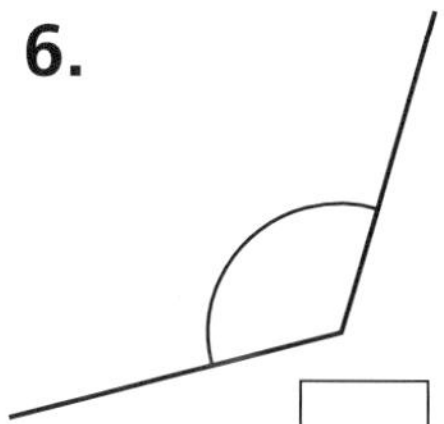

7.

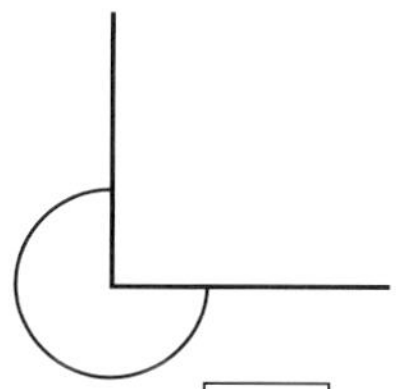

8.

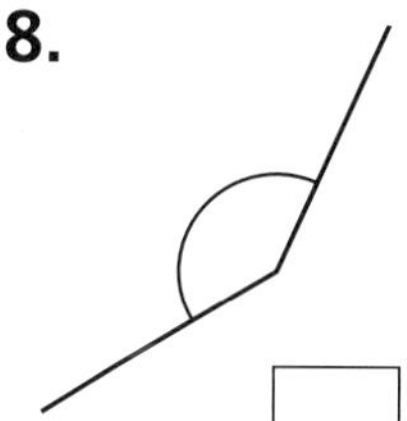

9.

10.

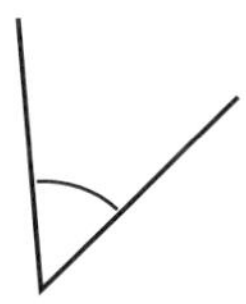

11.

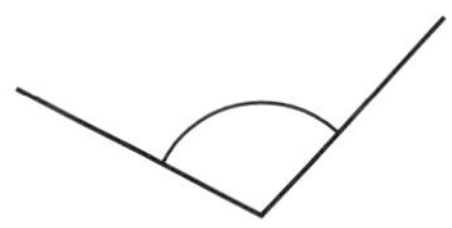

12.

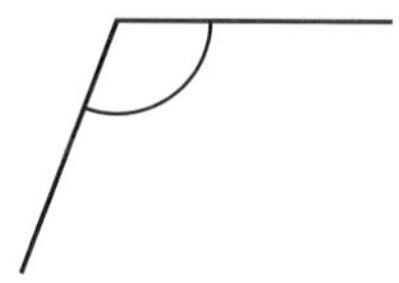

/5

13. Join the description to the correct shape.

a an irregular hexagon with three acute angles, two obtuse angles and a reflex angle

b an irregular hexagon with four right angles, an obtuse angle and a reflex angle

c an irregular hexagon with four acute angles and two reflex angles

d an irregular hexagon with two right angles, two acute angles and two reflex angles

e

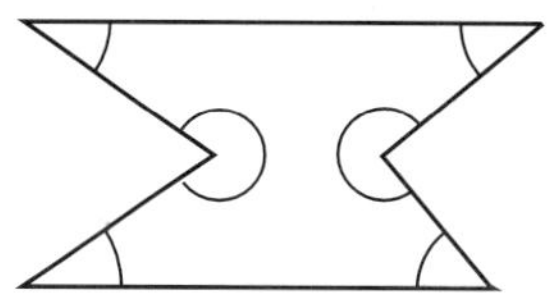

f

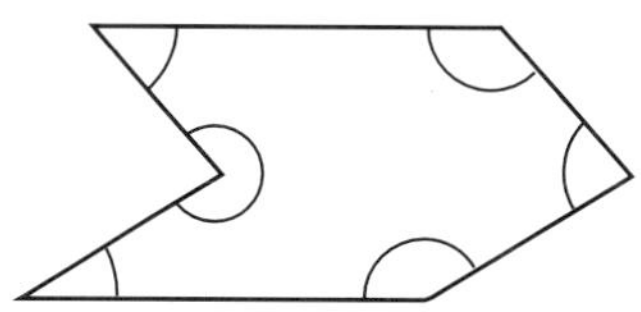

g

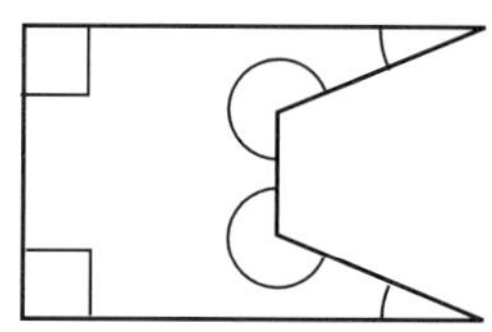

h

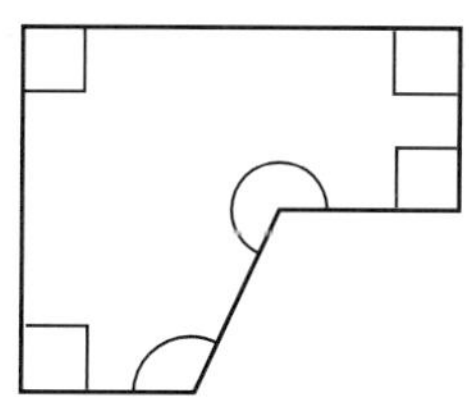

/4

Score: ☐ /13 Total: ☐

Bar-line graphs

Skills summary

- To draw a bar-line graph
- To extract information from a bar-line graph
- To use the mode and range of a set of data

Diagnostic materials

Shape, Data and Measures Textbook, page 57
- Check pupils can extract information from a bar-line graph.

Shape, Data and Measures Textbook, page 59
- Check pupils can construct a bar-line graph to show given information.

Oral questions

Pupils will need to look at the graph on their answer sheet.

1. How many children wore size 3 shoes?
2. Which shoe size is the mode?
3. How many children have a shoe size of 2 or smaller?
4. What is the range of the data?

Common difficulties

Pupils may find it difficult to read accurately from scales, especially if the scale is not marked in 1s but in 5s or 10s etc. Ensure pupils have plenty of practice in reading numbers from scales, particularly intermittent points. This may be developed through number line work. Encourage them to reason: *It is between 15 and 20, and is just over half way so it must be 18* etc. Pupils may find it useful to use a ruler to read across to the vertical axis, especially when reading the lines further away from the vertical axis.

Practice activities

1 Roll a dice 32 times and draw a graph of numbers rolled. Compare it to the one constructed from the information on page 59 of the Textbook.

2 Use two packs of playing cards with the picture cards removed. Shuffle the cards and pick 40 at random. Sort them and draw a graph to show how many cards there are of each number. Write questions that can be answered using the graph.

Answers

1. 5 **2.** 2 **3.** 12 **4.** 7
5. check the line has been drawn accurately on the graph
6. 64 **7.** 3 **8.** 12
9. check the lines have been drawn accurately

Name ______________________

1. [ ] **2.** [ ]

3. [ ] **4.** [ ]

/4

The number of children who had school dinners was recorded.

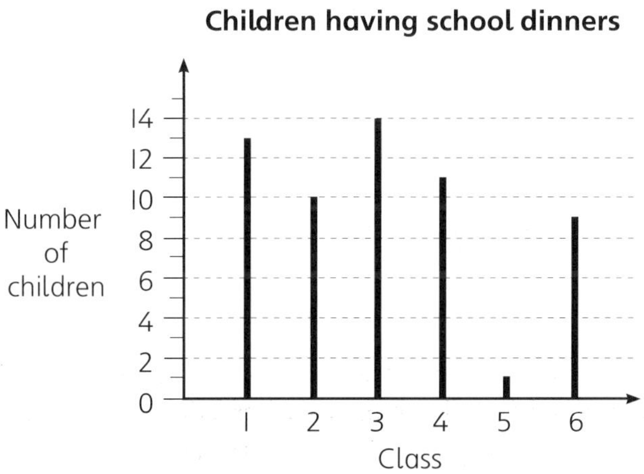

5. Six more children in class 5 have school dinners. Add them to the graph.

6. How many children have school dinners altogether? ________

7. In which class are school dinners most popular? ________

8. How many children in class 4 and 5 have school dinners? ________

/4

9. Complete the bar-line graph using the information in the frequency table.

Class	Frequency
1	5
2	8
3	9
4	4
5	7

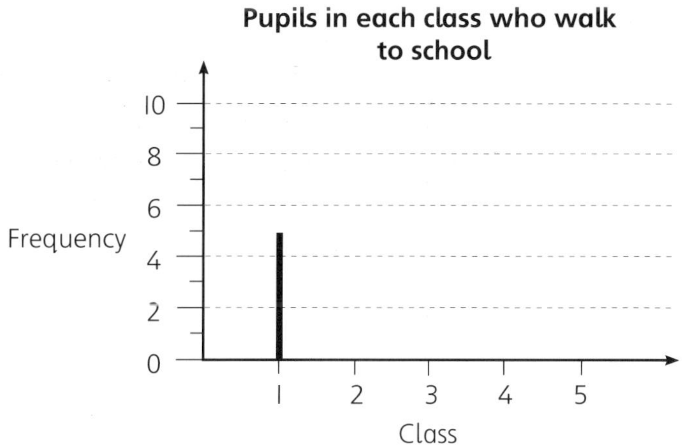

/4

Score: [ ] /12 Total: [ ]

Line graphs

Skills summary

- To extract information from line graphs where intermittent points have meaning
- To construct line graphs where intermittent points have meaning

Diagnostic materials

Shape, Data and Measures Textbook, page 60

- Check pupils can extract information from a line graph where intermittent points have meaning.

Shape, Data and Measures Textbook, page 62

- Check pupils are able to construct a line graph accurately from given information.

Oral questions

Pupils will need to look at the graph on their answer sheet.

1. What is the temperature at 9 a.m.?
2. What is the temperature at 11 a.m.?
3. How far does the temperature rise between 7 a.m. and 11 a.m.?
4. When is the temperature 6 °C?

Common difficulties

Pupils need plenty of practice in reading information from line graphs. They may find it difficult to read from intermittent points on both axes, e.g. reading the height of a balloon at 12:30 when the axes are marked in whole hours and 50 m divisions. Use a ruler to show pupils how to read from the horizontal axis up to the line of the graph and then across to the vertical axis. When constructing their own line graphs pupils need to be accurate. Use squared or graph paper and encourage pupils to use a ruler when joining points.

Practice activities

1 Take a reading on a thermometer. Put it in hot water. After 15 seconds take another reading. After a further 15 seconds take another reading. Take the thermometer out of the water and take a reading every 15 seconds until the thermometer shows the original temperature. Plot a graph of the results, with time across the horizontal axis and temperature up the vertical axis.

2 Find a line graph in a newspaper, perhaps in the travel or the financial section. Write two things that the line graph shows.

Answers

1. 4 °C	**2.** 9 °C	**3.** 7 °C	**4.** 9.30 a.m.
5. 1750 m	**6.** 12 noon	**7.** lunch/rest/no rise in slope	
8. 3 p.m.	**9.** check the graph has been completed accurately		

Name ________________

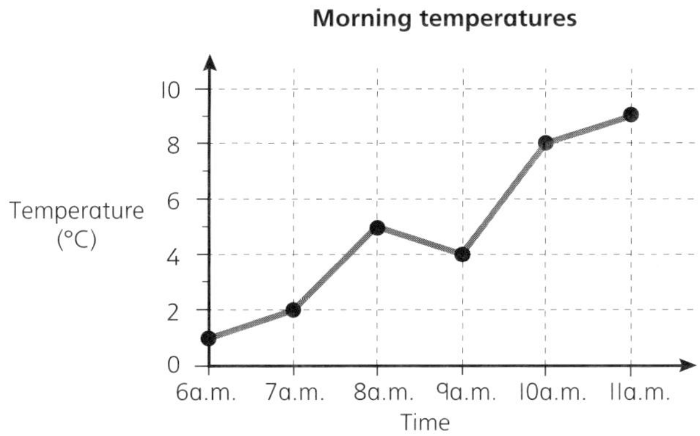

1. [ ] **2.** [ ]

3. [ ] **4.** [ ]

/4

This graph shows James' progress during a hill walk.

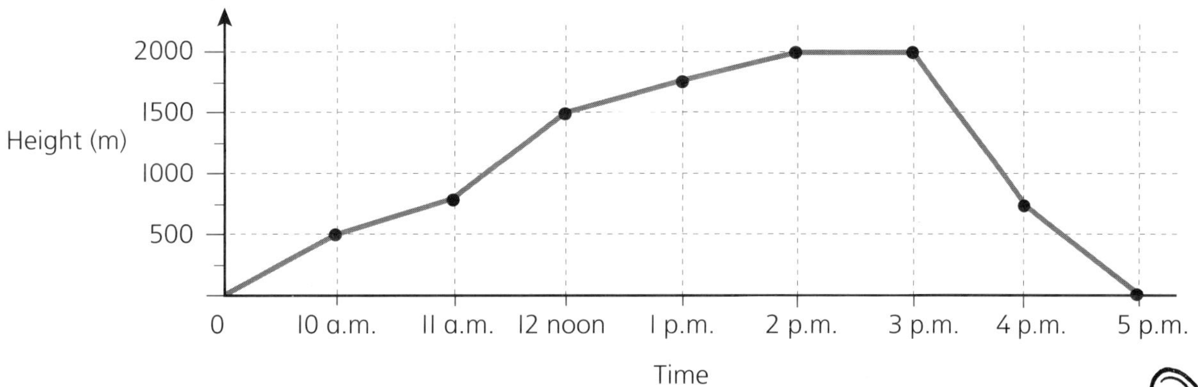

5. At what height is James at 1 p.m.? ________

6. What time is it when James reaches 1500 m? ________

7. What might be happening between 2 p.m. and 3 p.m.? ________

8. At what time does James begin to go down? ________

/4

Complete the graph using the data shown.

Time	**Height of bean**
1 day	1 cm
2 days	3 cm
3 days	6 cm
4 days	11 cm
5 days	12 cm

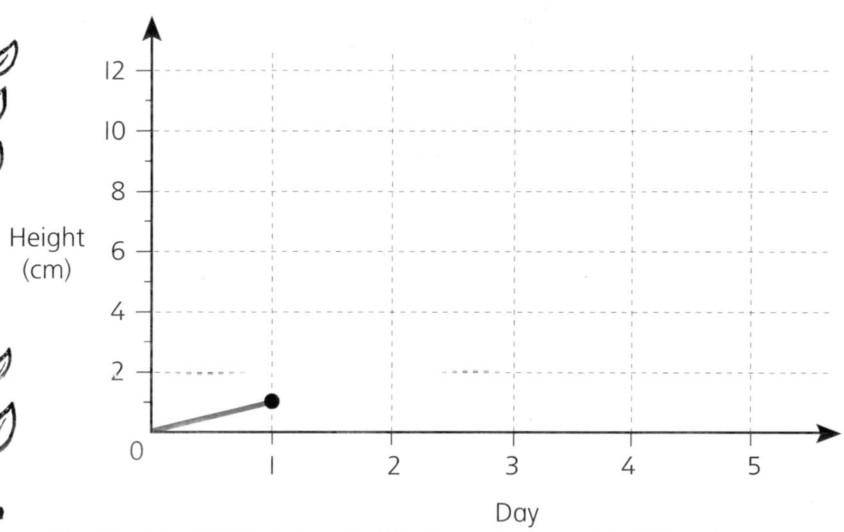

/4

Score: [ ] /12 Total: [ ]

Probability

Skills summary

- To classify events based on degrees of likelihood
- To use accurately 'impossible', 'unlikely', 'likely', 'certain'

Diagnostic materials

Shape, Data and Measures Textbook, page 63, questions 1 to 16

- Check pupils are able to decide on a degree of likelihood for given events by matching appropriate words to events.

Oral questions

Write true or false for questions 1 and 2.

1. It is unlikely that I am in a maths lesson.

2. It is certain that the school football team will win the F.A. Cup.

Write certain, impossible, likely or unlikely for questions 3 and 4.

3. I will come to school tomorrow.

4. The sun will shine next week.

Common difficulties

It is common for pupils to think events that they want to happen are likely rather than thinking about the *possibility* of it happening. Discuss with pupils what makes something likely or unlikely, referring to vocabulary they might be used to, e.g. 'good chance', 'poor chance'. Provide pupils with lots of practice in deciding the likelihood of events. Relate this to their everyday life, e.g. ask *Is it likely or unlikely that I will forget to set homework?*

Practice activities

1 Write down five things that you would like to do when you are older, each on a separate strip of paper. Order the strips of paper according to the likelihood of the event, with the most likely at the top.

2 At the start of the day write a list of things that might happen. Write 'certain', 'likely' or 'unlikely' next to each one. At the end of the day check through the list. Which events have happened? Which haven't happened?

Answers

1. false **2.** false **3.** answers depend on day of the week

4. likely or unlikely, depending on the time of year

6, 7 and **10** should be ticked **11.** check the order makes sense

Name ________________________________ **D3**

1. [ ] **2.** [ ] **3.** [ ] **4.** [ ]

/4

Tick the events that are unlikely.

5. going to bed tonight [ ]

6. having tea with the Prime Minister [ ]

7. snow falling in August [ ]

8. getting homework [ ]

9. the sun coming up [ ]

10. winning the lottery [ ]

/6

11. Put these events in order of likelihood. Put '1' by the most likely and '5' by the least likely.

I will watch TV today. [ ]

I will go on holiday to Mars. [ ]

I will remember everything I need for school this week. [ ]

I will play for Manchester United. [ ]

I will eat some chips this week. [ ]

/5

Score: [ ] /15 Total: [ ]

Record keeping

The record keeping grid list the units (or groups of units) assessed in this book. Across the top is room for up to fifteen names. Within each box on the grid is space to record the score each pupil achieved, so that over the course of the year you can easily track progress.

Names															
N1															
N2															
N3, N4															
N5, N6															
N7, N8															
N9															
N10, N11															
N12															
N13, N14															
N15, N18, N19															
N16, N17, N20															
N21, N22															
N23, N24, N25															
N26, N27															
N28, N29															
N30															
N31, N32															
N33, N34															
N35, N36															
N37															
N38, N39															
N40, N41															
N42, N43															
M1															
M2															
M3, M4															
M5															
M6, M7															
S1, S4															
S2, S3															
S5															
S6, S7															
S8, S9															
S10															
D1															
D2															
D3															